USING FILM AS A SOURCE

CW01095215

MANCHESTER
1824

Manchester University Press

IHR RESEARCH GUIDES

General editor: Miles Taylor
Series editors: Jane Winters, Simon Trafford and Jonathan Blaney

This series is for new researchers in history and is managed in association with the Institute of Historical Research (IHR). By offering a practical introduction to a sub-discipline of history, each book equips its readers to navigate a new field of interest. Every volume provides a survey of the historiography and current research in the subject; describes relevant methodological issues; looks at available primary sources in different media and formats and the problems of their access and interpretation. Each volume includes practical case studies and examples to guide your research, and handy tips on how to avoid some of the pitfalls which may lie in wait for the inexperienced researcher.

The guides are suitable for advanced final-year undergraduates, master's and first-year PhD students, as well as for independent researchers who wish to take their work to a more advanced stage.

USING FILM AS A SOURCE

SIAN BARBER

Manchester University Press

Copyright © Sian Barber 2015

The right of Sian Barber to be identified as the author of this work has been asserted by her in accordance with the Copyright, Designs and Patents Act 1988.

Published by Manchester University Press
Altrincham Street, Manchester M1 7JA

www.manchesteruniversitypress.co.uk

British Library Cataloguing-in-Publication Data
A catalogue record for this book is available from the British Library

Library of Congress Cataloging-in-Publication Data applied for

ISBN   978 07190 9030 1   paperback

First published 2015

The publisher has no responsibility for the persistence or accuracy of URLs for any external or third-party internet websites referred to in this book, and does not guarantee that any content on such websites is, or will remain, accurate or appropriate.

Typeset
by JCS Publishing Ltd, www.jcs-publishing.co.uk
Printed in Great Britain
by Bell & Bain Ltd, Glasgow

For my students, past and present,
who make it all worthwhile

CONTENTS

ILLUSTRATIONS

All images reproduced with permission from Photofest Digital

GENERAL EDITOR'S INTRODUCTION

Sian Barber's excellent introduction to film and history is a fitting first volume in the Institute of Historical Research's new series of research guides. The series aims to introduce first-time researchers to a field or sub-discipline of history and then navigate them through its historiography, methodology and opportunities for original research. Barber's guide does all this very effectively, giving the reader a firm understanding of the challenges but also the rich rewards and insights that arise from using film as historical evidence. As Barber emphasises, film is one of the most important and familiar cultural artefacts of the twentieth century: it both shapes and reflects the social and political contexts in which it is made, and the skilled historian needs to be alert to the technology and aesthetics of film in order to understand better what is going on when the screen becomes the source.

The volume provides a thorough introduction to history in film, and of the history of film as a source. Barber is careful to introduce the practical aspects of using film as evidence in historical inquiry. I anticipate that this volume will equip the reader to carry through the research process, from the first formulation of research questions to writing up findings for publication.

The Institute of Historical Research, University of London, has long been a provider of guides and research tools for historians. I am so very pleased that Sian Barber's volume is the first of a new series that will carry on that tradition.

Professor Miles Taylor, Director, Institute of Historical Research

ACKNOWLEDGEMENTS

I would like to thank everyone who has been involved in the production of this book, including everyone at Manchester University Press, particularly Emma Brennan and Rachel Winterbottom for their patience and professionalism. My thanks also go to Miles Taylor of the Institute of Historical Research, who commissioned me to write this volume, and to Jane Winters, who took time to read the original proposal.

This project would not have come to fruition without the support of colleagues and staff at Royal Holloway, University of London and Queen's University Belfast. It would never have been finished without the support of Sally Shaw, Ciara Chambers, Kim Akass and Cathy Johnson, who all provided much-needed solidarity. Finally, as always, my thanks to Paul, without whom none of this would have been possible.

GLOSSARY AND ABBREVIATIONS

180-degree rule	ensures that characters and objects remain on the same side of the frame. Inverting a scene or a shot within a sequence breaks this rule and the rules of continuity editing
auteur theory	dominant theory within film studies which suggests a single creative 'author' for a film text
chiaroscuro lighting	style of lighting which deliberately draws attention to shadows and light; often used to create strips of shadow across the frame
choker shot	shot of face or head which fills the whole frame
close up	head-and-shoulders shot
deep focus/ depth of field	action in a scene shown in sharp relief both in the background and the foreground
diegetic sound	sound in a film which has a source visible on the screen and which can be heard by the characters. Non diagetic sound can only be heard by the audience and is not heard by the character or present within the scene
Eady levy	tax levied on British exhibitors, who were required to repay a percentage of cinema admissions back to the producers of successful films
framing	how the action is arranged and shot
Hays Code	Hollywood production code which determined the content of American films
jump cut	a transition between shots which deliberately disrupts the expected narrative flow of a sequence

	by removing an expected shot or mis-matching two similar shots
leitmotif	a recurring musical cue which accompanies character or action
mise-en-scene	the organised contents of the frame and how the audience are invited to see it
montage	style of editing or combination of shots in sequence to achieve a particular effect
pan	camera moving horizontally on axis
shot/reverse	typical sequence of filmmaking shots often used for conversations and close ups
suture editing	(also known as continuity or invisible editing) brings individual shots and footage together without showing the joins. This ensures that the flow of a sequence is maintained and characters' eyelines, for example, remain at the same level
tilt	camera moving vertically on axis
verisimilitude	a crafted visual impression of reality

BBFC	British Board of Film Censors, founded in 1912, known from 1984 as the British Board of Film Classification
BECTU	Broadcasting, Entertainment, Cinematograph and Theatre Union
BFI	British Film Institute
BUFVC	British Universities Film & Video Council
NFFC	National Film Finance Corporation. Government body which supported the British film industry

Note: Use of bold though the text indicates key terms and ideas. Some of these are featured in the glossary but others are highlighted within the text to draw attention to key ideas as appropriate in individual sections.

1

INTRODUCTION

> The single most powerful obstacle to the historical use of film has been the historian's view that compared with the masses of other documentary evidence available film was especially unreliable as evidence.[1]

Film provides a fascinating insight into the past through documentary, archival and amateur film footage and a deliberately constructed historical world through feature films. However, using film as 'historical evidence' is far from straightforward; specific skills are required to understand the complexities of the visual medium, its relationship to the society from which it emerges, the industry which created it and those who consumed it. Despite these obstacles, film is a crucial means for understanding the recent past. William Hughes noted that 'the public's choice at the box office, provides a crude measure of the accuracy of the filmmaker's hypothesis about popular values', while Paul Smith considered that 'film records the outlook, intentions and capabilities of those who made it; it illustrates in some way the character of the society in which it was produced and for which it was designed'.[2]

Film is one of the dominant cultural forms of the twentieth and twenty-first centuries. What people chose to see and what filmmakers chose to make reveal a great deal about the nature of contemporary life, prevailing social concerns, preconceptions, morals and manners. Film can reveals a myriad of attitudes, not simply of those who are in the film, but also those of directors, scriptwriters, producers and financiers. Perhaps most importantly, films can help us understand how past audiences responded to issues, characters and ideals. Film and moving image can help us probe the delicate relationship between culture and society, between film and audience, and between spectators and the text. The films that are consumed by a society, the film stars venerated and the preferred genres, as well as trends in performance style, cinematography and costume, can all shed light on preoccupations of audiences in past decades.

The skills acquired in the fields of history, politics, English literature, sociology, cultural and media studies can all help to explore film as 'historical evidence', but the study of film is a discipline in its own right. Film cannot be treated simply as a historical source, but rather needs to be understood as a distinctive medium, possessed of visual and textual codes. This study guide is intended to provide a starting point for those seeking to use film as a source. It is aimed at those who want to use film and moving image as the basis for research and offers advice on research methods, theory and methodology and film-based analysis. Everything included here is also intended to be good practice, whether it be conducting an interview, visiting an archive, undertaking textual analysis or defining a research question.

It is likely that not all sections will be relevant for all readers; some may be interested in using film to explore political ideology, others may be interested in the study of feature films, while others may be keen to explore audience responses to particular groups of films. Film is a broad medium and as well as identifying the range of methods through which you can approach it, this work also indicates how works supplementary to film can be explored and utilised within research. With this in mind, this guide suggests how you can gather data on film audiences, identify and explore film industry documentation and locate personal papers of film industry insiders.

For many years film was *the* mass medium of education, communication and entertainment. Yet film's position has been eclipsed by the rapid growth of television and, more recently, the internet. While the medium of television operates under a different set of cultural imperatives, funding structures and production determinants, a great deal of what will be explored in relation to the visual qualities and research potential of film and its importance as a source can also be applied to television. However, television as a separate medium is not the principal focus of this work. This book will focus predominantly on film, and specifically on British films and the resources that pertain to this body of work. The focus is mainly British; Hollywood films are also referred to in passing, yet are not explored in significant depth or detail. The reason for this is twofold: firstly, to include a consideration of American resources would drastically increase the parameters of this work, and secondly, there are a great number of works which focus on Hollywood cinema and use Hollywood films as research examples. This work is intended to scrutinise British film culture and to offer ideas on how to explore, analyse, use and examine British films and cinema. The approach identified here for the study of British film, cinema and history can be applied to the different types of film produced and consumed anywhere in the world and so may be of use to students and scholars of any kind of film and moving image.

As well as being intended for those engaged in the study of film, this guide is also aimed at those who are keen to use film material in their research. There are many different ways in which film can be used to develop research, and the films themselves can either contribute to the overall topic of research or perhaps form the main body of the research material. For example, researchers might be keen to explore the visual representation of the 'blitz spirit' in British wartime film culture through newsreel footage or feature films, or to consider film propaganda in the extreme fascist regimes of 1930s. Perhaps the focus might be to examine changing masculinity in American films of the 1980s by focusing on stars such as Harrison Ford, Michael J. Fox and Tom Cruise. These research projects would require the researcher to use film in different ways. It is not simply a case of watching films to see what they are about and what they mean, but rather to analyse their textual qualities in detail, explore their production and reception contexts, and their relationship to industry and audiences.

It is also crucial to examine films in terms of their technical qualities and characteristics: films are both technical objects and a form of artistic expression, and this duality is crucial to fully understanding them. As James Monaco reminds us, 'every art is shaped not only by its political, philosophical and economic factors but also by its technology'.[3] It is not enough simply to concentrate on the aesthetic aspects of film; the researcher must also look at the technical factors in order to consider the impact of new editing, sound and cinematography techniques as well as special effects and computer-aided design.

Research into film could seek to understand film genres or movements further, to utilise film theory to explain the popularity of specific types of films in particular historical periods or to suggest a link between the visual culture of a decade and the preoccupations of the society which created and consumed it. It could seek to understand how industry and economics shape film products or explore how audiences responded to specific films or film events, such as *Star Wars* (1977), *Gone with the Wind* (1939) or *Alien* (1979). Research could focus on how newspapers respond to specific film texts such as the 'video nasties', or how film theorists understand and critique the work of Lars von Trier or

Jean Vigo, or how researchers seek to make sense of the use of history in films about the past.

In order to do justice to any of these topics, an understanding of film as an object is required. Film is a crafted artefact. It is rarely produced by a single person, but rather depends on the creative and technical skills of a range of people. It is also never produced in a cultural and social vacuum. It is both a product of a society and an object of consumption for society. Regardless of its genre and thematic preoccupations, film will always suggest something about the period in which it was made. Crucially, film is essentially a visual medium and analysis of visual style is a key part of understanding the film itself. Film and visual material does not just present straightforward narratives in simplistic ways. Historian J.A.S. Grenville observed that film is much more than simply a collection of images, noting 'the addition of a sound track can be made to influence the visual impact of what the camera shot. Montage or the art of film editing, can create the effects desired by the film maker.'[4] The study of film requires an understanding of all aspects of production, reception and visual style, and this work will suggest ways in which this can be achieved.

The first chapters of this book deal with the relationship that exists between history and film, film aesthetics and form, and film historiography. Chapter 2 considers the way in which the past has been created on screen and how film material has been used as a source to explore the past. In doing so it will suggest how even the most inaccurate, fictitious and crude filmic representations can be used to examine notions of the past and how such material should be approached. Chapter 3 will consider the characteristics that are particular to film as a source, specifically a visual source. It will demonstrate how to 'read' a film, to examine how the visual and textual language of films has been deliberately crafted and how it can be understood and explored. Chapter 4 will explore the trends that have informed film scholarship and the way in which film has been viewed, understood and studied in different periods. This chapter will also examine how trends in historiography can be discerned within and mapped alongside trends in film scholarship.

The next few chapters will move away from the theoretical and the historical and suggest a practical approach for studying film and using it as a source. Chapter 5 will offer suggestions on how to identify achievable research questions that draw upon and relate to film sources. It will indicate how research questions can be devised, how to begin working on a topic, and how to identify a useful approach. This chapter also includes two detailed case studies. Chapter 6 will follow on from the suggestions offered in Chapters 4 and 5 and demonstrate how a topic or research area can be matched with an appropriate methodology and a critical framework. Drawing on some of the key theories and approaches identified in Chapter 3, this chapter will also show how these theories can and have been used. The examples reveal how scholars working with film have utilised different critical and methodological approaches, and demonstrate the usefulness of existing work in helping to structure, research and approach your own film-related topic.

Chapters 7 and 8 relate to the resources that can be used to help explore and understand film. Chapter 7 will offer a detailed survey of the specific kinds of resources available, where they are held and how they can be accessed. This exploration will include conventional resources such as books and academic journals, but will also contain information about primary sources, archival material and the extensive digital collections that are accessible. Chapter 8 suggests ways in which the different sources can be used. Examples here will draw upon newspaper material, account books and ledgers, personal papers and interview transcripts. The chapter will also suggest how such material can be interrogated, for example how film reviews can be read and understood, how interviews should be conducted, how to access visual or written material in an archive and the value of online fan sites. Finally, Chapter 9 offers ideas on how research can be written up, the kind of information which should be included in essays or research projects, how the analysis should be written, what tone you should adopt, how your work should be structured and the way in which material should be referenced.

The book aims to provide the tools to undertake film-related analysis. While ambitious in scope, this work cannot hope to cover everything. Detailed explorations of new media, television, amateur films and YouTube content can all be found elsewhere and will only be mentioned here where relevant. This guide is intended to be of use for film and media studies undergraduates and also for those who use film as part of advanced research who may not have studied the subject before. It will aim to provide answers to the following questions:

- How do I identify source materials?
- How can I analyse my material?
- What critical approach should I adopt?

- How do I devise a methodology?
- What are the best sources to use in film analysis?
- Do I need to visit an archive?
- How should I structure my work?

As well as offering answers to these questions, this guide also situates film-related research work within a tradition of academic scholarship and deliberately challenges outdated notions of film as an unreliable historical source. This work does not set out to reinvent the wheel; there are a large number of excellent works which address the topic of film as a historical source, including recent publications on film and history by James Chapman, Martin Pereboom and Marnie Hughes-Warrington.[5] In addition to work which is specific to the discipline of film studies, there are also numerous useful publications which address how historians make use of moving image. Within such publications, the idea of film as a source is usually addressed, though the textual specificities of the film medium are sometimes overlooked in a desire to align film with more conventional sources. This work intends to address both issues; it will suggest how to conduct film-related research and also offer guidelines on both textual analysis and the use of supplementary evidence which extends beyond the text itself. This work refers to the work of others in appropriate detail, but in the sections where the sources noted are illustrative, the texts and authors are mentioned only briefly. This is to prevent the inclusion of a range of sample sources within the text itself and bibliography.

Some readers may also feel that the archive and archival film research included here receives greater attention than textual analysis. This is due to both the intention of this work to foreground the uses of film as a source and the need for a work which provides a useful starting point for those keen to explore film-related archive material.

NOTES

1 J.A.S Grenville, *Film as History* (Birmingham: University of Birmingham Press, 1971), p. 4 (inaugural lecture delivered in the University of Birmingham, 5 March 1970).

2 William Hughes, 'The evaluation of film as evidence' in Paul Smith (ed.), *Film and the Historian* (Cambridge: Cambridge University Press, 1976), p. 71; and Paul Smith (ed.), *Film and the Historian* (Cambridge: Cambridge University Press, 1976), p. 7.

3 James Monaco, *How to Read a Film: The World of Movies, Media and Multimedia: Language, History, Theory* (New York and Oxford: Oxford University Press, 2000), p. 49.

4 Grenville, *Film as History*, p. 17.

5 James Chapman, *Film and History* (Basingstoke: Palgrave Macmillan, 2013); Maartin Pereboom, *History and Film: Moving Pictures and the Study of the Past* (Upper Saddle River, NJ: Pearson, 2010); Marnie Hughes-Warrington, *History Goes to the Movies: Studying History on Film* (London: Routledge, 2007).

⇒ 2 ⇐

FILM AND HISTORY

> The peculiarity of historical films is that they are defined according to
> a discipline that is completely outside the cinema.[1]

When thinking about film as a source, one of the key questions which
emerges is the film's relationship to the past it represents and how
films operate as historical objects. The relationship between film and
the historical past is a curious one and so this chapter will explore a
number of different approaches available to the researcher to better
understand this relationship. Firstly, this chapter will briefly consider
the ways in which the historical past is presented on screen and the
challenges this can pose to the historian. Films never present the past in
a straightforward way and so different approaches to character, narrative
and period need to be delicately probed. Secondly, the importance of
films as historical sources will be discussed. This section will consider
the range and importance of different types of moving image and
their usefulness to contemporary historians. As well as feature films
about the past, documentary and archive footage, amateur footage and
newsreels will also be briefly examined and their relevance for historians
critiqued. Thirdly, this chapter will suggest ways in which historians can
use moving image in mindful ways and the key questions which should
be considered when undertaking analysis of moving image material.

The last section includes two distinct case studies which indicate
different ways to explore the relationship between history and film.

THE HISTORICAL PAST ON SCREEN

Big-budget feature films such as *Robin Hood: Prince of Thieves* (1991),
Braveheart (1995) and *Pearl Harbor* (2001) are frequently ridiculed for
presenting inaccurate or fictitious accounts of the past. But this kind
of historical film has less to do with history as an academic discipline

and more to do with making narratives of the past accessible and entertaining for audiences. As John Tosh has observed, 'when the past is conserved or re-enacted for our entertainment, it is usually presented in its most attractive light.'[2] Films noted for their cavalier treatment of the past, including those mentioned above, are usually highly conventional in filmic terms. They obey all the rules of classical filmic storytelling – narrative, structure, character, plot resolution – and it is in terms of filmmaking, rather than in terms of history, that these films should first be evaluated.

For all their grandiose claims for historical accuracy and authenticity, historical films can never offer an interpretation of history 'as it really was' and are rarely trying to attempt such a feat, preferring instead to focus on a version of history which can be sold to audiences. We can use films to explore what versions of the past are preferred by audiences, how and why films use the historical past to entertain or to educate, and how history is used to allay contemporary fears.

Historical representations may range from the reverential to the ribald, from cavalier to camp and mocking to melodramatic. However, even films which deal with the past in farcical, comical and irreverent ways are not useless or unworthy of study, nor can it be said that such films simply present 'bad' history. *Carry On up the Khyber* (1968) may say little about British India, but says a great deal about attitudes towards British imperialism, colonialism, race, gender and ideas of comedy and national identity in late 1960s Britain. Sometimes it is the treatment and handling of the historical subject that is most interesting, rather than historical accuracy.

Representations of the past will also differ according to the period in which they are made. For example, Kenneth Branagh's 1989 adaptation of Shakespeare's *Henry V* is a very different film to Laurence Olivier's much-lauded 1944 imagining. Although both films are drawn from exactly the same source text and follow the same narrative with the same characters, visually they are very different. Olivier's version was made at the height of the Second World War in 1943 and released into cinemas in 1944. As James Chapman has shown, wartime audiences would have appreciated the war narrative, while the need for the film to be positive and upbeat accounts for its lack of bloodshed.[3]

By contrast Branagh's 1989 adaptation is dirty, gritty and viciously bloody. Scenes from the original play that were removed from Olivier's version such as Henry's decision to execute the prisoners, Henry's doubts on the eve of battle, and the King's aggression and warlike demeanour are all present in Branagh's interpretation. Made over forty years later, the Branagh film has a very different purpose and would have been seen by audiences far more used to graphic depictions of warfare. Since the conclusion of the Second World War, televised wars, including Korea, Vietnam and the first Gulf War, had presented audiences with glimpses of modern warfare. The Branagh film builds on this tradition; the fighting scenes are graphic and visceral and depict behaviour – including the pillaging of corpses on the battlefield and the slitting of throats of enemy soldiers – which would never have featured in a film made in 1944.

It is also crucial to remember that Shakespeare's *Henry V* cannot be seen as an accurate historical portrayal but rather a piece of Tudor propaganda which itself needs to be scrutinised as a historical source. Any discussion of the film adaptations would have to take note of the versions of history at work in both the filmic interpretation and within the original play. Issues of adaptation loom large in discussions of history on film. If exploring historical adaptation, you need to consider if the film is based upon a novel such as Margaret Irwin's bestselling *Young Bess*, a poem such as Tennyson's 'The charge of the Light Brigade' or a play like *Oh! What a Lovely War*.

Films adapted from pre-existing material have a further layer of authorship that needs to be acknowledged and explored. The past is never simply being recreated but rather it is being interpreted. A screenwriter may be adapting an earlier source text into a film, but to what extent is the author of the source text then influential in shaping the film itself? For example, the swashbuckling adventures of *Tom Jones* (1963) are based on the novel by Henry Fielding and set in the eighteenth century. While the character, narrative and setting are Fielding's, the film's visual style, costumes, performance and music must all be seen through a filter of the period when the film was made and are the result of deliberate choices by the filmmakers, screenwriters, actors and technical crew. The film is a costumed romp which incorporates traces of the heady, sexually liberated and vibrant 1960s and blends them with the historical past to create a film for contemporary audiences. Albert Finney swaggers across the screen as Fielding's eponymous hero, fighting, drinking and fornicating with scant regard for period trappings.

Similarly John Schlesinger's *Far from the Madding Crowd* (1967) also takes a traditional literary narrative and brings it to the screen in sun-drenched, colour-saturated glory which cannot but remind audiences of the 'swinging 1960s' rather than evoking the more muted nineteenth-century settings described in Thomas Hardy's original novel. In Joseph Losey's *The Go-Between* (1971), the grand houses and wide outdoor spaces are bathed in slightly sour sunlight, while the modernity of the character's mannerisms and the way in which the dialogue is delivered sits awkwardly alongside the period costumes and setting. The anxieties of 1970s femininity are evident within the film and the casting of 30-year-old Julie Christie as L.P. Hartley's 19-year-old heroine Marian only adds to the awkwardness which pervades this heritage-infused drama of life and loss.

One of the most interesting issues with adapting the past is how filmmakers return to the work of certain authors again and again. Suzanne Pucci and James Thompson suggest that the constant return of both filmmakers and audiences to Jane Austen and the Regency period has a great deal to do with nostalgia for an imagined past, the mediation between past and present and the residual cultural capital of Austen's work which continues to make her world and its character's relevant for modern-day audiences.[4]

The adaptation of Jane Austen's *Emma* into the high-school comedy *Clueless* (1995) shifts the prescriptive Regency society satirised by Austen to modern-day Beverley Hills. Within this adaptation the teenage protagonists are preoccupied with clothes, scandal, sex and popularity – concerns that also dominated Regency society. In this way the Regency past is made relevant for modern audiences, specifically young cinemagoing audiences familiar with high-school comedies. This self-conscious contemporary feel, which Andrew Higson identifies, is not confined to Austen but can also be discerned in updates of Dickens and Shakespeare. Films made in this period include: Baz Luhrman's *William Shakespeare's Romeo and Juliet* (1996); *10 Things I Hate About You* (1999), which is an update of *Taming of the Shrew*; *O* (2001), a modern-day interpretation of *Othello*; and *Great Expectations* (1998), re-imagined by Alfonso Cuarón.[5] Making the past relevant for teenagers is a key feature of all of these films and while their settings may not be historical, the historical source material makes these modern-day adaptations important contributions to the broad church of historical and heritage films (see fig. 1).

While there are crossovers, it is important not to conflate ideas of heritage and of history; heritage carries with it a set of expectations that often bear little resemblance to more conventional history. Andrew Higson contends that 'one of the key characteristics of the modern English past represented in costume dramas ... is the display of heritage spectacle, in terms of landscape, architecture and interior design'.[6]

1 Shakespeare reworked; Patrick Verona (Heath Ledger) woos feisty Katarina Stratford (Julia Stiles) in *10 Things I Hate About You* (1999)

Within this category he includes the lavish Merchant Ivory adaptations such as *Room with a View* (1985) and *Howards End* (1992), country-house period dramas such as *Remains of the Day* (1993) and *Shadowlands* (1993) and the Austen adaptations. To this group we could also add television dramas like *Upstairs Downstairs* (1971–1975), *The House of Elliott* (1991–1994) and *Downton Abbey*,(2010–present) which all share a similar heritage aesthetic and narrative preoccupations.

These films and programmes are focused on representing a period aesthetic to make the past appealing. Regardless of the activities of the characters and the development of the narrative, it usually takes place within the confines of a specifically imagined and lovingly recreated historical world of wealth and privilege. Such films focus on the lives of the wealthy and well-born, and the narrative is usually preoccupied with money, marriage and class. A heritage film does not need to communicate or represent a complex historical past but rather simply presents a beautifully crafted world. Yet, in order for these films to be understood, well received and popular, the world they recreate needs to be instantly recognisable to audiences. The popularity of British heritage cinema, both in Britain and beyond indicates the consistent and residual appeal of this specific representation of the past, but how can these kind of films be understood and used as historical sources in their own right?

THE MOVING IMAGE AS A SOURCE

As well as being artistically created objects, films are also artefacts which offer evidence of an historical past; that is, the past in which they were made rather than the period in which they are set. J.A.S Grenville has observed that the 'reality' which films present is 'rearranged to suit the filmmaker's artistic, social or political intentions' and that filmmakers can banish temporal and spatial limitations through a variety of different techniques.[7] When Grenville wrote about using film as evidence he was predominantly concerned – as were the majority of modern cultural historians – with documentary film, specifically with film footage which captured 'real' events and used 'real' people. Tony Barta confirmed this historical preoccupation, noting how 'writers of scholarly history remain unenthusiastic about a cinematic comparison: film is still easier to see as either an authentic (recorded) past or a fake (acted) past'.[8]

In 1980, Pierre Sorlin boldly challenged the assumptions that newsreels and documentary film footage were authentic, asserting instead, 'we are obliged to treat newsreels as 'distorted' or rather as directed images of society'.[9] Today, in our mediatised world, much of what we absorb as part of our everyday lived experience is specifically generated for the purposes of being seen, and many, if not all, of our media experiences are directed. The way in which we experience visual culture has also changed: films are now available to download, television runs for twenty-four hours and can be paused, recorded and replayed, while the internet offers a seemingly endless stream of moving image and has become the ultimate viewing and sharing platform for user-generated material.

While the experience of watching and viewing has changed, the material which is now so easily available remains a useful cultural indicator and can be effectively used to explore the preconceptions and concerns of modern society. Our understanding of the importance of visual culture as a historical and cultural source has deepened, yet discussions about the unreliable nature of feature film and moving image as historical evidence persist, with moving image material constantly cited as a flawed source. Ignoring the potential of using films as sources misses the point that all sources are flawed, and that moving image sources simply need to be treated with the same rigorous investigation as traditional sources. Ludmilla Jordanova has pointed out, 'inevitably some documents are more reliable, less overtly mediated than others, but all, by their very nature, are nonetheless mediations'.[10] Film – whether a cinema newsreel, a documentary with an overt political agenda, a light 1930s musical comedy or the latest installment in the Harry Potter franchise – must be evaluated in terms of its objective and bias as well as its content, aesthetics and form. In this way films are no different from conventional written sources.

Sorlin suggested that, while newsreels offer filmed and selected views of the past, feature films possess much more inherent value as they are texts which are produced by an industry and consumed by audiences. He argued that it is this relationship between production and reception which makes feature films so fascinating as historical evidence, as they can be used to explore contemporary mores, manners, expectations and attitudes.[11] But does this make the moving image less reliable than other sources? Robert Rosenstone acknowledges that the discipline of history involves privileging specific narratives, representing particular points of view and focusing on key events to explore wider issues. In this way he suggests that to a certain extent written narratives are 'verbal fictions' and concedes that 'visual narratives will be "visual fictions" … not mirrors of the past but representations of it'.[12] This is the case for all films, not simply those which are set in or about the past. All films offer a representation of reality, but film is not, and never can be, a mirror of society.

Another charge levelled at representation of history on film is that through the grand narrative of storytelling, elements which are held so dear to historians are overlooked, specifically historical nuance, conflicting accounts and the importance of historical evidence. Rosenstone considers that the straightforward narrative strategy deployed in many conventional historical films 'denies historical alternatives, does away with complexities of motivation or causation, and banishes all subtlety from the world of history'.[13]

Is this really the case? Film as a form can offer a multiplicity of meanings and interpretations, and this ambiguity shares a great deal with the nuance and subjectivity which is so important to the discipline of history. Film is not without nuance and many films can and do utilise their storytelling capabilities in meaningful ways; for example, documentary films frequently use filmmaking techniques to address particular issues, while in earlier periods political ideology has been anchored in individual films in order to present a particular view of the past. The epic films made by Sergei Eisenstein such as *Battleship Potemkin* (1925) and *Oktober* (1928) provide an insight into both contemporary Soviet society and also highlight key events from the historical past. Through his use of montage, editing and sound, Eisenstein offers a critical historical perspective, which illuminates Soviet filmmaking in the 1920s and the political ideology which underpinned the production of his films.

Just as filmmaking can be political, thoughtful and nuanced, audiences also respond to films in informed and thoughtful ways. The 'meaning-making' power of the audience has frequently been overlooked in critiques of film, with experts deploring historical inaccuracies and suggesting that audiences will accept the mythologised and often fantastical worlds presented on screen as 'fact'. But this is to underestimate the capabilities of both audiences and filmmakers. Tony Barta suggests that the hostility of historians to filmic representations of the past has more to do with anxieties about the discipline of history itself. He observes that 'instant history on the screen fore-grounded "history" the process – as unstable and open', perhaps suggesting that allowing hoi polloi without historical training to access the past in such a way permitted audiences to engage with the past in a way which was not dependent on historical scholarship.[14] Modern audiences are film savvy, highly aware and heavily critical. They are also carefully attuned to filmic conventions and tropes, particularly those used to present the past, such as the framing of the past through the lens of the present with characters looking back on past events and accompanied by flashbacks or voiceovers, or the accessing of the past through a historical object such as a diary, a painting or letter.

It is also important to note that films are not the only sources that claim to present unbiased 'truth'. Diaries, personal accounts, financial ledgers, newspaper articles, interviews, witness statements, official proclamations and many other sources make grandiose claims for historical authenticity and accuracy. We should never accept any of these sources at face value but rather be sceptical of what they claim to do and carefully evaluate the source. All sources have bias and films are no different. As William Hughes points out, with film as with other sources we must be concerned with the familiar problems of dating, authorship, point of view, authentication and verification.[15]

Along with documentaries and news reports, feature films can also seek to offer 'authentic' versions of the past by incorporating real filmed footage of past events or drawing on other visual imagery. The lavish biopic of Queen Victoria, *Sixty Glorious Years* (1938), uses well-known paintings, engravings and portraits to recreate set-piece tableaux such as the marriage of Victoria and Albert, Victoria in mourning and the Queen and her family visiting the Crimean War wounded in hospital. Using existing source material in this way creates a sense of authenticity and familiarity within the mise-en-scene. The opening sequences of *This is England* (2006) also reference a historical past, but in a different way. Director Shane Meadows uses historical news footage of events such as the election of Margaret Thatcher and British National Party marches to create period authenticity and to locate the narrative firmly within a specific timeframe. It also serves to make audiences aware of key events such as the Falklands War which are so important to the development of the film's narrative.

It is also important to think about the context in which these films offer their retelling of the past. For example, the Biblical epics produced in 1950s Hollywood relied on extensive sets, a vast budget and a cast of thousands. This cycle of films drew upon classical antiquity – Ancient Greece, Rome and Egypt – for their films about the past. Films of this type included *The Robe* (1953), *The Ten Commandments* (1956) and *Ben-Hur* (1959). Hollywood's decisions to focus on a distant past and far-away lands allowed for a presentation of the exotic otherness of the past and to sidestep both the USA's own relative lack of history and its more contentious history, notably slavery and civil war as well as contemporary anxieties such as the McCarthyism which stalked Hollywood.

Just as the past is not 'fixed', neither is our interpretation of it. Andrew Higson has suggested that within films, 'different aesthetic and ideological traits, different cultural traditions and identities are adopted to represent different pasts and appeal to different audiences'.[16] Unlike academic history, films are deliberately intended to appeal to audiences and, in exploring films set in the past or about the past we need to think about what audiences need to know and understand. The past on film is made relevant for audiences for a variety of different reasons. Pierre Sorlin notes:

> The cultural heritage of every country and every community includes dates, events and characters known to all members of that community ... it is enough to select a few details from this for the audience to known that it is watching a historical film and to place it, at least approximately.[17]

In this way, he argues, historical film allows historians to establish the 'basic historical knowledge' of a society and explore the way in which that knowledge is communicated, developed, challenged and confronted through the film medium.[18] Peter Burke also noted that cultural history enables the 'translation' of the language of the past into that of the present, making the past 'both visible and intelligible'.[19] This is certainly the case with the historical film, which strives to make the past accessible for film audiences, but just as we cannot speak of 'the past' it is also difficult to generalise about 'the historical film'. We need to consider what kind of historical film it is. Is it a costume film, a literary adaptation or a heritage film? Is it a grandiose historical epic or a low-budget romp? Does it base its relationship to the past upon a source text, a novel, painting, person or series of historical events? And how is it using historical material; does it tell a story, is it being used to locate a specific narrative, does it provide period detail or authenticity, or is it being used to reflect upon the past?

HOW TO USE THE MOVING IMAGE
AS A HISTORICAL SOURCE

Film is not like written history and its purpose is not simply to educate or to inform. Its purpose is generally commercial entertainment and in order for a film to be a success the subject matter, narrative and characters need to be appealing in a competitive market. The lives of fourteenth-century peasants, eighteenth-century workers, failed revolutionaries destined for anonymity, plantation slaves or oppressed citizens may not be obvious box-office draws and it can be a challenge to make these narratives appealing to cinema audiences. One way in which to enliven such tales of minority groups is to fictionalise aspects of these narratives and thus move away from the solid foundations of history and into the realms of historical fantasy.

Films can often be most interesting in what they do not show; for example, the information that is implied in set design, music or costume but never said. If the past is being presented in a particular way, the researcher's job is not to bemoan the lack of authenticity evident in the period detail, but to ask why the past has been reconfigured in such a way. We should consider: who the film is aimed at, what were the intentions of the director, what were the influences on the set and costume designers. All films offer a range of viewing pleasures for their audiences and it is important to recognise the specific experiences that clothes, music, dialogue, character and narrative offer in different kinds of historical films and films which use the past. All questions about the ways in which the films construct a historical past need to be framed around general questions of what the film is trying to do and how it is doing it.

As with all scholarship, film sources need to be interrogated and their probity challenged. In order to use any film as a source, we must ask how it has been created, why it has been created and who it has been created for. We need to examine what it presents and what is suggested through the narrative but we should also look for omissions, obfuscations and absences within the text. Are the anachronisms deliberate, or simply the result of poor research?

Different films visualise the past in different ways and, as Natalie Zemon Davis points out, there can be many pitfalls in a visualised historical past. She draws attention to 'obtrusiveness or staginess of props or costumes' which can obscure the historical period and the narrative but she also considers that an overdone period look can render a film 'static' and emotionless.[20] Stanley Kubrick and his cinematographer John Alcott drew inspiration for his adaptation of Thackeray's *Barry Lyndon* (1975) from landscape paintings by Lawrence and Watteau, while the influence of the portraits executed by Lawrence and Gainsborough can be seen in the visualisation of the courtly characters in Derek Jarman's reworking of *The Tempest* (1979). But what does this kind of attention to historical detail suggest about the production of the film and the creative personal behind it?

Money is a key factor in film production and the costs behind any film reveal a great deal about its intended audience and how it is being positioned in the market. If the film is intended to tap into the heritage market and the production has a substantial budget, then it is likely that the setting will be lavishly authentic with a high level of attention to detail. Stately homes have stood in as key locations in a range of historical films from *Gosford Park* (2001), *Vanity Fair* (2004), *Atonement* (2007) and *Jane Eyre* (2011) with production designers making use of the magnificent exterior and interiors of locations such as Castle Howard and Chatsworth to create a 'look' of the past but also to suggest class or wealth through the set dressing and the resulting mise-en-scene. Information about film locations and the specific look desired by set designers and cinematographers can often be found in magazine and newspaper articles and provide a useful insight into the reasons behind the choice of specific locations.[21] As well as location filming, researchers should think about how the sets have been constructed. Are they well crafted and realistic looking? Is more suggested by the set than simply historical accuracy or location setting? A clever set designer will make the film set suggestive of far more than simple historical period. Artist Derek Jarman famously designed the city walls of seventeenth-century Loudun in Ken Russell's adaptation of *The Devils* (1971) to look like a public lavatory. The grubby white tiles not only provide a sordid and degraded backdrop to the narrative of religious corruption which unfolds but also fit in with the source material in which Aldous Huxley declared that the exorcism of Sister Jeanne was similar to 'a rape in a public lavatory'.[22]

We also must consider if the past is being fashioned for a particular purpose – for example, to appeal to a modern, young audience. Does the dialogue sound authentic or is it anachronistic? Does it sit well with the rest of the film or does it jar with the film's visual style? Is everyone speaking with cut-glass English accents or in drawling American tones? Has there been an effort to make the characters sound as if they come from a different era? Is regionality expressed in the accents of individual characters and, if so, does this relate to class, status, wealth or background? Is music used within the film to create a period feel? Is it music from the time in which the film was set – for example, classical pieces which may be recognisable to audiences – or is it deliberately anachronistic to challenge ideas of historical authenticity? For example, the anachronistic touches in Sofia Coppola's *Marie Antoinette* (2006) include the use of pop music on the soundtrack and shots of modern trainers underneath hooped ball-gowns. Such deliberate touches need to be considered as part of the film's mise-en-scene and seen as evidence of the specific decisions made by set and costume designers. Other questions to ask could be: has the music been specifically composed for the film and if so, who composed it? Are a variety of musical pieces included? Do characters within the film contribute to the musical aspects of the film by playing an instrument as part of the narrative? Piano performances feature heavily in heritage films and period dramas and the music used and the way in which it is delivered is often heavily linked to character. It is important to remember that sound includes much more then simply music: what sounds can be discerned on the soundtrack and what kind of setting, mood or feeling do they evoke?

Case study:
the Tudors on film

This case study will look at representations of the Tudor dynasty and the range of ways in which these historical figures have been explored. As Sue Harper reminds us, 'History can carry an infinite range of meanings and societies regularly reformulate it for current use.'[23]

Films which depict the same historical character but which are produced in very different periods offer an insight into the expectations of different audiences. For example, Cate Blanchett's Elizabeth I is very different to portrayals of the Virgin Queen by Glenda Jackson, Bette Davis or Flora Robson.[24] The grandiose style of Robson, the imperious theatricality of Davis and the political astuteness of Jackson indicate different aspects of the same fictional character, but also draw attention to the different periods in which these successive films were made and the modern concerns which may have shaped audiences' responses. As a further contrast, Miranda Richardson's simpering Queenie in the BBC television series *Blackadder* (1986) offers yet another portrayal which needs to be viewed in the traditions of heavy satire favoured by this programme.

Similarly, representations of Henry VIII also vary widely and include the serious and sombre portrayals of a monarch battling with his conscience and preoccupied with the fate of England, to the sex-obsessed and bad-tempered Henry of the Carry On series memorably caricatured by Sid James in *Carry On Henry* (1971). Recent historical representations have focused unashamedly on Henry's love life, with *The Other Boleyn Girl* (2008) dwelling on the bedroom antics of the monarch as he is caught between two sisters. A similar approach is taken within the BBC television series *The Tudors* (2007–2010), which focuses upon the sex and scandal of the period. Such an approach picks up on the promise implicit in Alexander Korda's *The Private Life of Henry VIII* (1933) but delivers far more graphic and salacious material due to altered notions of acceptability, relaxation of censorship and changes in attitudes towards monarchy.

Interpretations of the past are less about historical accuracy and more about entertainment, costumes, visual style, character and spectacle. We need to search for nuance and implication in the mise-en-scene, in precisely the same way that historians search for nuance and subjectivity in sources. As Natalie Zemon Davis has wondered: 'How then is historical authenticity conceived in the common parlance of the film world? Most frequently it is a matter of the look of the past or rather "the period look", "period props" and "period costume".'[25] We must consider how much attention has been given to period detail in the film, what the costumes and textures are like. Are they historically accurate or do they look overdone and ornate or alternatively cheap and unrealistic? What kind of colours have been used within the set? If it is a Tudor-set piece then there is likely to be a great deal of red and gold to fit in with period detail drawn from iconic contemporary paintings by Holbein and Hillier.

It is also helpful to think about conditions of production; Hollywood's take on the Tudors will be very different from a British re-imagining. This may be in part due to the amount of money which studios have to spend, but will also say something about audiences and who the film is intended for. For example, is it a big-budget epic which will appeal to the widest possible audience, or it is a heritage production which is targeting the art-house audience? We also need to think about the specifics of the past being shown. For example, is the film about Henry VIII gaining a divorce from Catherine or Aragon and breaking with the Church in Rome to marry Anne Boleyn, as in *Anne of the Thousand Days* (1969) or *A Man for All Seasons* (1966), or is the Tudor setting simply the location for some historical romping? (see fig. 2).

One of the difficulties in analysing uses of the past on film is finding critical responses that move beyond simplistic notions of historical accuracy and authenticity. One film reviewer dubbed King Henry VIII in *The Other Boleyn Girl* as 'nothing more than a gullible sex addict in wacky shoulder pads'.[26] Yet to dismiss a film for being historically inaccurate is unhelpful. *The Other Boleyn Girl* was made as a lavish big-budget production and featured A-list Hollywood stars Natalie

2 Tudor magnificence in *Anne of the Thousand Days* (1969), starring Richard Burton as Henry VIII and Genevieve Bujold as Anne Boleyn

Portman, Scarlett Johansson and Eric Bana. Based on a bestselling and popular novel by Philippa Gregory, the film's principal preoccupation would have been to appeal to as wide an audience as possible and to present the historical characters as modern individuals to appeal to and resonate with a modern audience. Such a film could never include a level of historical detail and accuracy which would please historians, and the film blends together a few facts with historical fiction to showcase the appeal of the past through scandal, intrigue, sex and drama.

We also need to consider whether the narrative is based on 'real' events or is a fictionalised account, a missing chapter or a 'secret history' of a prominent individual. John Madden's *Shakespeare in Love* (1998) takes a great deal which we do know – Stratford-born playwright, royal patronage, *Romeo and Juliet* and bawdy Elizabethan humour – and mixes it with fictional elements, a love affair which inspired one of Shakespeare's famous plays and a selection of invented characters, as well as modern and anachronistic touches which appeal to modern audiences. Mention of Anne Hathaway's cottage – a key part of the Shakespeare tourist trail – and the rivalry, implied plagiarism and shared writing experiences with Christopher Marlowe nod towards the knowing in the audience who may be concerned with debates in Shakespearean scholarship about the authorship of the plays. But for the most part, the film is a historical romantic comedy. Like many other historical films of this type, shared cultural knowledge will enhance the audience experience but the film can, of course, be understood and appreciated without it. In this way, the film is using history and our knowledge of the past in a range of different ways in order to appeal to different audiences.

Case study:
real footage/real events

As well as fiction films which use all the methods of conventional cinema to create a fictionalised historical past, the past also emerges on film in other guises. The twentieth century exists within newsreel footage, amateur moving image collections, news broadcasts and documentary. All of these different forms will have sought to capture the past for different reasons. A documentary filmmaker may have followed a collection of railway workers, as in Harry Watt and Basil Wright's *Night Mail* (1936), or else captured the actions of schoolchildren or celebrity-hungry exhibitionists, as in *Educating Essex* (2011) or *Big Brother* (2000–present). Frequently, such material seeks to capture everyday life, real people or events and to present images of life 'as it was'. Such an objective is, of course, problematic as the very act of filming something ensures that it is no longer real. Material such as that captured in Dziga Vertov's *Man with a Movie Camera* (1929) indeed documents real life and mundane events within the working day, but the footage has been carefully edited together; someone has made choices about what to include and what to exclude. On a more fundamental level, someone has also made the decision to turn the camera on and begin filming. Just because the material may have been shot of real people and real events – such as the famous Mitchell and Kenyon material of factory workers and fair-goers – it does not mean it is straightforward and authentic. It must still be interrogated as a crafted and created source.

As well as exploring material deliberately shot for documentary purposes, it is important to consider how and why other moving image material may have been captured. Newsreels shown in cinemas were often used to highlight recent events and items in the news, and in times of war or hardship, the tone of such material will be deliberately patriotic and positive. News from the front would have provided important (although heavily censored) information to those back home, while government-made shorts such as *Britain Can Take It* (1940) documented the impact of the Blitz on London and were used to stiffen the resolve of citizens on the home front. Similarly, images of cheering crowds seeing soldiers off to fight in 1914 offered a recruiting opportunity and a means of galvanising enlistment.

Such collections of filmed material raise questions about how the past and how 'real life' are being captured and preserved on film. How will they be used in the future? One of the most common ways in which archive or newsreel footage is used is its inclusion in later documentaries or programmes. Ken Loach's *Spirit of '45* (2013) uses a great deal of archive footage of post-war Britain and the first days of the NHS and combines it with recently conducted interview material, voiceover, captions and point-of-view narration. Yet the original archive footage was not shot to be included in this particular documentary. Loach has selected it and fashioned it to create his own film and we must be aware of this reuse. We need to consider if the moving image exists as part of a collection, if it is broadly available online or by appointment only. Such factors will always inform how it has been used and by whom.

Documentaries and newsreels present factual images of the past, but frequently such footage is used out of context or comes to represent something quite different. For example, grainy black-and-white images of uniformed soldiers marching across the muddy, shell-torn fields of Flanders or Belgium have become generic short-hand for the carnage of trench warfare during the First World War. Similarly, footage of fighter planes in the sky against a backdrop of falling bombs – whether it is newsreel footage or shots from films as varied as *The Way to the Stars* (1945) or *Memphis Belle* (1990) – can be used to suggest the Battle of Britain. It is important to understand that the version of history being presented in this 'factual' format has being deliberately crafted for audiences to understand. The footage used in documentary programmes or feature films will be presented in a particular way, to draw attention to certain things.

As well as thinking about how such material can and has been used, we need to consider the context. Is this the only material of a particular event which exists? If not, then why is this the case? Has other material been lost, or was there only a single camera to document the event? If little footage exists, then how have filmmakers accounted for this omission? Have they staged re-enactments in order to make the shots more dramatic, as was the case with the footage showing men going over the top in the propaganda documentary *Battle of the Somme* (1916)? And how does this problematise notions of 'authenticity' or 'reality'?

In the same way that we must delicately and methodically explore fictionalised accounts of the past, we must also be aware that factual or semi-factual moving image is not a straightforward and unproblematic source either. It must also be carefully evaluated and its contents, context and purpose thoroughly explored.

CONCLUSION

All films which deal with the past are useful for the historian, but they cannot simply be viewed as re-enactments of the past captured on celluloid. They need to be understood within the broader concepts of production and reception and interrogated as relevant yet flawed historical sources. The following chapter will suggest how films can be analysed and how their different elements must be examined in order to best understand their meanings.

NOTES

1   Pierre Sorlin, *The Film in History: Restaging the Past* (Oxford: Basil Blackwell, 1980) p. 20.

2   John Tosh, *The Pursuit of History*, 4th edition (Harlow: Pearson Education, 2006), p. 17.

3   James Chapman, *Past and Present: National Identity and the British Historical Film* (London: I.B. Tauris, 2005), pp. 113–142.

4   Suzanne R. Pucci and James Thompson, *Jane Austen and Co: Remaking the Past in Contemporary Culture* (Albany, NY: State University of New York Press, 2003).

5   Andrew Higson, *Film England: Culturally English Filmmaking since the 1990s* (London: I.B. Tauris, 2011) pp. 191–192.

6   *Ibid.*, p. 208.

7   Grenville, *Film as History*, p. 17.

8   Tony Barta (ed.), *Screening the Past: Film and the Representation of History* (Westport, CT: Praeger, 1998), p. 12.

9   Sorlin, *The Film in History*, p. 15.

10   Ludmilla Jordanova, *History in Practice* (London: Hodder Headline, 2000), p. 97.

11   Pierre Sorlin, 'The film in history' in Marnie Hughes-Warrington (ed.), *History on Film Reader* (Abingdon: Routledge, 2009), pp. 15–16.

12   Robert A. Rosenstone, 'History in images/history in words' in Hughes-Warrington (ed.), *History on Film Reader*, p. 37.

13   *Ibid.*, p. 31.

14   Barta (ed.), *Screening the Past*, p. 5.

15   Hughes, 'The evaluation of film as evidence', p. 49.

16   Higson, *Film England*, p. 192.

17   Sorlin, *The Film in History*, p. 20.

18   *Ibid.*

19   Peter Burke, *Varieties of Cultural History* (Cambridge: Polity Press, 1997), p. 193.

20   *Ibid.*, p. 18.

21   Cathy Whitlock, 'The grand estates and castles of period moves', *Architectural Digest* online, www.architecturaldigest.com/ad/set-design/2013/period-movies-set-design-manors-castles-vanity-fair-jane-eyre-article (accessed 15 October 2014).

22   Aldous Huxley, *The Devils of Loudun* (London: Chatto & Windus, 1952), p. 132.

23   Sue Harper, *Picturing the Past: The Rise and Fall of the British Costume Film* (London: BFI Publishing, 1994), p. 1.

24   Cate Blanchett played Elizabeth I in the film *Elizabeth* in 1998, Glenda Jackson played the role on television in *Elizabeth R* in 1971, Bette Davis played the Queen twice, first in *The Private Lives of Elizabeth and Essex* in 1939 and again in *The Virgin Queen* in 1955, while Flora Robson was Elizabeth in *Fire over England* in 1937.

25   Natalie Zemon Davis, 'Any resemblance to persons living or dead: film and the challenge of authenticity' in Hughes-Warrington (ed.), *History on Film Reader*, p. 17.

26   Alex von Tunzelmann, '*The Other Boleyn Girl*: Hollyoaks in fancy dress', *Guardian*, 7 August 2008, www.guardian.co.uk/film/2008/aug/07/1?INTCMP=SRCH (accessed 15 October 2014).

RECOMMENDED FURTHER READING

Barta, Tony (ed.), *Screening the Past: Film and the Representation of History* (Westport, CT: Praeger, 1998).

Chapman, James, *Film and History* (Basingstoke: Palgrave Macmillan, 2013).

Hughes-Warrington, Marnie, *History Goes to the Movies: Studying History on Film* (London: Routledge, 2007).

Landy, Marcia (ed.), *The Historical Film: History and Memory in Media* (New Brunswick, NJ: Rutgers University Press).

Rosenstone, Robert A., *History on Film/Film on History* (Harlow: Pearson, 2012).

Smith, Paul (ed.), *Film and the Historian* (London: Cambridge University Press, 1976).

Sorlin, Pierre, *The Film in History: Restaging the Past* (Basil Blackwell: Oxford, 1980).

Stubbs, Jonathan, *Historical Film: A Critical Introduction* (London: Bloomsbury, 2013).

❧ 3 ❧

FILM FORM AND AESTHETICS

This chapter offers an introduction to film analysis. Although this work emphasises the importance of film as a cultural and historical object, it is crucial to recognise the textual specificity of film. As the work is partly aimed at those who may not have studied film before, this chapter will outline how to explore visual style and will draw attention to how this is constructed through lighting, staging, performance, camerawork, costumes and music.

The focus here is film and, while the examples are predominantly drawn from feature films, it is helpful to think of the notion of 'filmed material' as including a broader range of moving image. Such an approach will allow for the inclusion of amateur film, television material and newsreel footage. Of course, some of the suggestions for ways to analyse feature film might not be appropriate or applicable for newsreel footage or YouTube clips; in these cases it is unlikely that detailed mise-en-scene analysis will be helpful. However, all filmed material shares some basic characteristics. Filmmakers, regardless of whether they craft big-budget feature films or small vignettes captured on a mobile phone, make choices about how to shoot and what to include. The majority of filmed material is created to be seen and so analysis of the moving image should always consider the particular purpose of the material and who it is or was intended for. One of the major differences between types of filmed material is budget. The budgets of most feature films far exceed those of television programmes – although some television drama series such as 2013's *The White Queen* are undeniably lavish – and production context and methods of working also differ. This chapter will suggest ways in which film and filmed material can be analysed and understood and how such analysis can be undertaken in a methodical manner.

THE SPECIFIC QUALITIES OF FILM MATERIAL

Film possesses unique qualities and characteristics. It is not enough simply to see films as poor relations of written texts, yet many methods of historical analysis consistently favour written rather then visual material. The reasons for this are mainly historical. As Sarah Barber and Corinna Peniston-Bird have pointed out, 'the document became the core tool of historical interpretation and defined the responsibility of historical practitioners'.[1] Yet film is not a document; as already shown in the previous chapter even close and faithful visual adaptations of works of literature are different from their source material and so pose different questions for the researcher. What can take pages to describe in a novel can be captured in a few brief establishing shots within a film or television drama. Such shots can establish location, period, time and setting and communicate all of this to an audience before a single word has been uttered. It is not only production, script or direction which can aid the translation of a text onto the screen; costume can reveal detail about class, status, background and wealth; lighting can flatter or obscure characters and settings; editing and montage can document the passage of time, a transformation or a number of events unfolding simultaneously, while techniques such as voiceover or flashbacks are particular filmmaking techniques which lend themselves to the telling of a story in a visual way. Identifying the specific qualities of the visual medium is the first task of the film scholar, while the second task is to explore how such effects are being achieved and what impact they have.

WHAT IS IT AND WHO MADE IT?

Before beginning any analysis, it is important to consider what the filmed material is. Is it a feature film produced by a Hollywood studio? If so, we will already know a great deal about it. It will be easy to get hold of basic information such as cast, director, budget, release date, production costs and box-office performance. It should also be fairly simple to get hold of a copy of the film itself. If it is a less well-known film or one which has yet to be released on DVD this information and the film itself may be harder to track down. If it is a television programme then some information will be more pertinent; we will need to know when it was made, when it was broadcast and on what channel. We should also ask if it was part of a series, a piece of commissioned drama, light entertainment or investigative journalism. All of this information will help us to understand what the programme is, who it is intended for and how we need to consider it. If the footage is part of an amateur film collection then the job is harder still and research will depend upon the cataloguing details preserved and the knowledge of librarians and archivists who may have specific information about the collection as a whole. If the footage is something you have discovered online then it may be difficult to identify what it is; you will need to explore the site on which the material is hosted to gather some basic information and then check this information with other sources. When using online material, you should gather as much information as possible, including URLs and details of the host site and the date you accessed it. This will help when you come to reference the material. How to use online, digital and archival sources will be covered in Chapter 8.

Once you have identified the material, you now need to consider who made it. Very few films are the product of a single person's work; even amateur films often involve a number of people. Television and feature films frequently require a crew of hundreds; if there are special effects or animation involved, this can become thousands. The work of the director, the producer, cinematographer, costume and set designers, camera operator, editor, lighting team, animators, stunt crew, the cast and many more combine to create a film's specific 'look'. When critiquing films and seeking to understand their composition and creation, it is important to look at the individual elements which combine to create the finished product.

Many useful introductory guides exist to help scholars and researchers to interpret the visual elements of films. They include those by James Monaco (*How to Read a Film*), Timothy Corrigan and Patricia White (*The Film Experience*), David Bordwell and Kristin Thompson (*Film Art: An Introduction*) and Pam Cook and Mieke Bernink (*The Cinema Book*). These textbooks offer useful examples to illustrate how different visual, textual and aural elements can be explored. All of the elements which can be discerned within finished films fall into two basic categories; the elements which are part of the production process and those which are added during post-production. However, there may be some overlap. For example, camerawork and filming are part of the production process, but the selection of specific shots and the decisions on how to bring them all together are part of editing, which counts as post-production. The rest of this chapter will focus on the specific elements which can be analysed and draw attention to how these different elements work together. It is important to explore the separate elements but also to acknowledge how the disparate elements contribute to the overall process of film production.

CAMERAWORK

A good place to begin film analysis is with camerawork and to ask what the camera is pointed at, how the action is being framed, what kind of distance, focus and perspective are being used, how the camera is moving and what effect all this has.

The position of the camera informs what audiences see and from whose point of view they see it. It also has a profound influence on how audiences respond to characters, locations and narrative. As James Monaco points out, 'the most salient difference between staged drama and filmed drama, as it is between prose narrative and film narrative, is in point of view'.[2] In only permitting the audience to look at part of the action, by refusing to let their gaze wander to anything outside the sight of the camera, the filmmaker deliberately and consciously determines the focus of the audience. The enormous range and seemingly endless options offered by a profusion of cameras and shots cannot disguise the fact that viewers are being shown what the filmmaker desires them to see. Even within documentary film, the idea of an objective camera is a myth; someone has looked down the viewfinder and selected the angles, chosen the setting, the depth, the focus and the range of the desired shots.

The way in which the camera is being used depends on what kind of camera it is. If it is fixed in one location, as it is for some filmed television drama and for set scenes within feature films, the camera remains stationary, moving on an axis, tilting up and down or from side to side. **Pan shots** where the camera stays fixed in one location and moves side to side helps to survey a scene, follow the movement of the actors within the frame and provides a sense of space and of scale. **Tilting** up and down creates low and high camera angles; tilting upwards can make characters appear more important or menacing, whereas high camera angles which are titled down will have the opposite effect. If the camera is not fixed but rather is shoulder-mounted then it will have greater ease of movement. Mobile cameras such as the steadicam allow good-quality footage to be shot from a camera which has the freedom to move about the set, capturing a broader range of angles, following characters, tracking them and creating an entirely different visual effect to that achieved with a static camera. As filmmaking techniques have developed, filmmakers have established new ways of capturing footage – mounting cameras on cranes or helicopters, on specially built dollies, and building tracks so that the camera can run alongside the action. A high crane shot can be seen in *Gone with the Wind* (1939) when Scarlett enters the yard full of wounded Confederate soldiers. The shot begins with a close up of Scarlett and then slowly pulls back from her to reveal more and more wounded soldiers on the ground until the camera placed high atop the crane is surveying the scene from a distance. The chase scenes in John Ford's *Stagecoach* (1939) were filmed by a camera which ran on tracks alongside the coach and which allowed for moving footage to be captured. Key sequences in *A Taste of Honey* (1961), one of the British new wave films, are filmed using a hand-held camera, which captures the cramped interiors of the working-class homes and factories in a way which would not have been possible with a fixed camera. *The Blair Witch Project* (1999), a low-budget independent horror film, used hand-held cameras deliberately to create an amateur style to the film, a novelty which contributed to its box-office success.

Sometimes it is immediately clear what kind of camera is being used and why, at other times this can only be discovered through visual analysis supported by additional research into production. It is always useful to think about the way the footage is being shot and the impact and effect this has. Does it make us as the audience feel more detached or more involved? If the camera is following a character closely and tracking their every move, do we feel more attached to the character? Or if the camera is fixed in an interior location and simply observes interaction between a range of characters, does it make us more or less involved in the scene which is unfolding? Does the camera keep a respectful distance from the action or is it up close so that we can see every tear, frown or smile?

Depth of field is the term used to describe filming which allows for action taking place deep within a scene to be brought into sharp relief. Action occurring in the foreground can be juxtaposed with detail in the background. For example, two adults can be seen having a conversation in the foreground while children sleep or play in the background. Depth of field is cleverly utilised in Powell and Pressburger's *A Matter of Life and Death* (1946) where the scenes on the heavenly staircase incorporate the earthly life-saving surgery in the foreground watched over by the heavenly judge and jury (as well as by Peter and June) in the background.

Shots

As well as where the camera is placed and how it is moving, you should also identify the kind of shots which are being used. Cinematography with its specific shots should always be considered alongside editing, but for the purposes of clarity, they are separated here. **Wide shots** are frequently used to capture open spaces, landscapes and vistas. Any western will have a plethora of wide shots, while **aerial shots** are also used to indicate scope and scale and are often the opening shots of a film. The opening camera shots in *The Sound of Music* (1965), which swing around the lush green hills before coming to rest upon the figure of Julie Andrews, were captured by a camera mounted on a helicopter. Other films, perhaps with smaller budgets, content themselves with static establishing shots.

Most films begin with a shot which establishes location, period, time and setting; for example, a wide open shot of the prairie of the American Midwest with houses and homesteads, or a sweeping vista of mountains, or a quiet suburban street. An establishing shot is usually followed by a medium shot, of a single house in a street, for example. The final shot in this series is the medium close up – the camera moves in to highlight the specific focus of the action or the narrative. It might track a figure walking up the street, or pass through a window or door to the family inside. As well as establishing location and setting, opening shots can also be coupled with a voiceover. David Lean's *This Happy Breed* (1944) begins in such a way; after a series of establishing shots of the terraced streets of London, the camera then shifts to focus in on the back gardens of the terraces and finally moves through the window into the home of the Gibbons family. All of this is achieved through a series of slow-moving rather than static shots.

Once the location and setting have been established, camerawork will usually focus on characters. The most common sequence of shots is designed to follow dialogue and at the same time to capture characters' responses. For example, regardless of whether a character exchange is taking place in soap opera or in a feature film, the sequence of **shot/ reverse shot** is used time and time again. Conversations are played out between two characters facing one another and are captured by two cameras, each one placed behind the shoulder of each actor. A good example of this is the ball sequence in *Sense and Sensibility* (1995) where Marianne confronts Willoughby. The two cameras behind the shoulders of each protagonist allow the audience to capture the reactions of both characters as well as the occasional glimpse of Elinor as an unhappy spectator. This sequence of shot/reverse shot is repeated for the duration of the conversation until Willoughby moves and then the camera tracks him walking away and then cuts back to the anguished face of Marianne, while Elinor moves into the frame to comfort her sister.

When analysing any sequence of moving image material it is important to think about where the camera has been placed and what impact this has upon us as the audience. Do we feel part of this conversation? Do we feel as if we are intruding, or is it being staged for our benefit? How are the events being framed? Are there other characters in the scene who are watching these events take place and are we seeing the events through their eyes?

Point-of-view shots are a key way of creating character identification; they encourage us to wonder where the camera is positioned and who is doing the looking. Are we looking at the characters when they are speaking, or when they are thinking, or when they are reacting to something? What effect does this have and whose perspective are we viewing it from? Is the point of view fixed, or does it shift, and do our sympathies or interests shift along with it? You should also consider how far away the camera is from the action. Is the scene made up of **long shots** or **close ups** or perhaps a mixture of both? Does the camera remain the same distance from the action or are **zooms** employed to capture emotion or responses at key moments? Are there any extreme close ups or **choker shots**, which contain only the faces or eyes of the characters and document their expressions in acute detail? What is the purpose of these deliberate choices?

EDITING

Once filming has been completed, this material will be edited. Editing which brings individual shots and footage together without showing the joins to the audience is a process known as **suture**, **invisible** or **continuity editing** and is the most common form of editing within mainstream and commercial cinema. These editing practices are part of the standards and norms established in classical Hollywood narrative. With suture editing, the eyelines of individual characters are matched up carefully, so to achieve a sense of reality and not to distract or disorientate the viewer with technical inconsistencies.

Within conventional shooting and editing, certain standards are observed, specifically that relating to the practices of shot/reverse shot identified above, but also in relation to ideas of perspective. It is standard practice in conventional or mainstream cinema for cameras not to break the **180-degree rule**. This maintains that shooting of characters, locations and events will be from the front and that there is an invisible line which they will not cross and is an acknowledgement of cinema's theatrical roots. Adhering to the 180-degree rule means that there will be consistency within a particular scene; the camera will not suddenly show characters positioned in the right-hand side of the frame, seconds after they have been shown to be on the left-hand side of the frame. Such shots could be easily achieved with camera movement or multiple cameras but would break the invisible barrier which exists between the audience and that which is being shown. It would deliberately challenge the audience and flout the idea that what is being shown is real. It would also disrupt the narrative flow that is another characteristic of classical Hollywood filmmaking. Of course, filmmakers can deliberately break these established conventions and in doing so often challenge the audience, forcing them to acknowledge that what they are seeing is a 'construction' rather than a reality.

Challenges to editing conventions take a variety of different forms. During the 1920s Soviet filmmakers Sergei Eisenstein and Dziga Vertov challenged the practices of editing which sought to disguise the construction of the film and advocated using cinematic montage as a style of editing. Eisenstein considered **montage** to be a 'collision' or a 'conflict' and this style of editing can be seen in his historical epics like *Battleship Potemkin* (1925). Classical editing techniques were also challenged by French new wave filmmakers, notably Jean-Luc Goddard in his seminal film *Breathless* (1960), which avoids straightforward editing in favour of frequent **jump cuts** to disorientate and challenge the viewer. A jump cut is a transition between shots which is not smooth but deliberately disrupts the expected narrative flow of a sequence; it removes a shot from the expected sequence of shots, or deliberately places two similar but non-matching shots alongside one another to create a 'jump' and to disorientate the audience.

Analysis of the camerawork and of the editing techniques offers an insight into how the film or scene has been put together, but all of these technical elements must be explored in relation to how the overall filmed material looks and what actually appears in the frame.

MISE-EN-SCENE

Mise-en-scene is the creation of the world within the cinema frame crafted specifically for the spectator of the film. It comprises many different elements and for clarity these elements will be addressed separately. When looking at the overall effect of the mise-en-scene you need to be able to identify how the different elements are working together and what overall effect is being created. If the film is a realist narrative which takes place in a modern setting, does the mise-en-scene create a sense of reality, of **verisimilitude**? Do we believe what we see or are there elements which appear jarring or ill-fitting? When beginning analysis of mise-en-scene we should consider how the different visual and verbal codes of a film are working with one another: are they working together, or in opposition to one another? Are the colours too bright, or the music too loud, the performances of the characters too melodramatic or the backdrop in too sharp a focus? Is this effect the result of clashes between creative personnel on the set, or is it a deliberate choice to imply something that is not explicitly addressed in the narrative? For example, films made in Hollywood at the height of the Hays Code used filmic mise-en-scene to suggest sexual relationships or behaviour which could not be overtly addressed in the text. Douglas Sirk's melodrama *Written on the Wind* (1956) uses the lushness of the visual detail and the meanings implicit in the hotel room in which Kyle installs Lucy to indicate what cannot be directly addressed within the scene itself – specifically the precise nature of what he is offering her. All of this is communicated through the artfully arranged flowers, immaculately displayed clothes and intimate accessories as well as the way in which the scene is flooded with artificial light and the soft yet cloying pastel colours of drapes, curtains and bedspreads.

When analysing mise-en-scene you need to consider what elements are part of the production process – for example, costume, performance, setting and lighting – and what elements have been added in post production – for example, music and editing. The rest of this section will now consider the separate and distinct elements of mise-en-scene.

Setting

Firstly, where are the scenes being shot? Is it a variety of locations – interiors and exteriors? Are these lavish or on a strict budget? Has any money been spent on locations and is this visible in the film? For example, Stanley Kubrick spent a vast amount on *Barry Lyndon* (1975) to achieve a distinct period feel, while Lawrence Olivier's *Henry V* (1944) featured location filming with contemporary Ireland standing in for medieval England. By contrast, the Carry On films frequently filmed exterior shots in the car park at Pinewood Studios, including the Spanish beach scenes in *Carry on Abroad* (1972). For *Carry On Cleo* (1964) the production team were able to borrow the massive Egyptian sets constructed for 20th Century Fox's *Cleopatra* (1963) the previous year and by reusing the expensive scenery keep their own production costs down.

You should consider the level of detail included within the sets. Is it detailed or bare? What can we see? Can we make out distinct objects, fabrics, furniture, textures? Or does it all blend together to create an atmosphere of poor taste, wealth, poverty or ostentation? A clever and well-executed set design will also offer something of character background. Interior locations will show how characters live and provide them with a past and a present. The dripping walls and poorly lit cramped spaces of *Vera Drake* (2004) evoke poverty, deprivation and poor sanitation. But the locations also suggest a tight-knit working-class community and a visual evocation of the urban inner city in the 1950s, as well as the social realism popular in earlier periods of British filmmaking. Sometimes the set design is less about a naturalistic evocation of place and space and more about mood or tone. Films which are fantastical or futuristic frequently eschew set designs which evoke realism. In Tim Burton's *Edward Scissorhands* (1990), the gothic castle, the pastel-coloured suburban houses and Edward's cleverly executed topiary combine to create a diverse and visual fantasy land for the spectator.

If the sets have been constructed, think about how this has been achieved. Many of the sets for the locations in Peter Jackson's sprawling Lord of the Rings trilogy were based on a series of detailed scale models which were then filmed and edited together with live-action performance and CGI. But this was only possible due to the film's enormous budget and major studio backing. Other films have far fewer options. In *Monty Python and the Holy Grail* (1975) the Python team had very little to spend on the film and instead of trying to hide their lack of budget drew attention to it using coconuts to represent clip-clopping horses and filming on location to reduce studio costs.

Lighting

Lighting a film is a technical skill which can help to set mood and tone, present characters in a particular way and determine the focus of a scene. You should consider whether the scene is lit from above or below. Where is the source of the light, and does it fall evenly onto the set or are there pools or bars of light discernible in specific scenes? Do some parts of interior or exterior locations remain in darkness? Keeping part of the set only partially lit works particular well within horror films; dark shadows allow predators to lurk and then suddenly emerge to terrorise their victims. Lighting frequently works to enhance the set design and cinematography; for example, in the *Cabinet of Doctor Caligari* (1920) the lighting both adds to the atmosphere and draws attention to the cleverly crafted, angular and cubist-inspired set design. Deliberately drawing attention to angles and shining lights through interior features such as window blinds, stair banisters and window frames to create strips of shadow is known as **chiaroscuro lighting**. This particular style of lighting is characteristic of German expressionist films such as *Caligari* or *Nosferatu* (1922) and found its way into Hollywood films through the work of émigré directors like F.W. Murnau and Fritz Lang and came to mainstream prominence in the film noir genre. The complex, twisting narratives of noir were a good fit for chiaroscuro lighting with its clever use of shadows and depth to enhance the darkness of plot, character and setting. In films such as *Double Indemnity* (1944), *Scarlet Street* (1945) and *The Big Sleep* (1946) we can see these distinct lighting and camera elements working together to produce a particular aesthetic effect and to enhance narrative and character development.

When analysing lighting you should consider if the entire film looks the same, or if the lighting shifts and changes to create particular moods. Is the lighting harsh or soft? Is it tinged with blue, yellow or green undertones? Lenses and filters applied to the cameras can help to create a particular lighting effect. The visual style of *Barry Lyndon* is soft and painterly and its interior sequences are carefully lit to evoke the texture of candlelight and of the historical period (see fig. 3).

Contemporary-set films such as *Mean Girls* (2004) are brash, bright and vivid in their colour palette. Here the lighting draws attention to the conspicuous consumption and teenage preoccupations of the characters. In *The Truman Show* (1998) the fictional town of Seahaven is bathed in artificially bright sunshine. The harsh and sharp lighting contributes to the staginess of the location and this becomes more

3 Period set dressing, costumes and lighting in *Barry Lyndon* (1975), with Ryan O'Neal as the eponymous hero

evident throughout the film, culminating with the 'sun' being revealed to be a giant spotlight which the all-seeing and sinister executive producer turns upon the hapless Truman as he tries to flee. In Derek Jarman's *The Tempest* (1979), blue filters were applied to the cameras for the filming of all the exterior shots to create deliberately washed-out sequences and to make it visually clear that Prospero's island was no tropical paradise drenched in lush technicolour. By contrast, the island sequences in *South Pacific* (1958) bathed the set in deep orange light for some of the important emotional and musical moments in the film and to foreground the dreamlike and romantic elements in the narrative.

Music and sound

The soundtrack of a film is essential to create mood and to link disparate scenes. Think about how the soundtrack of the film has been created – does it include background noises; if so, what can you identify? Can you hear car noises, train whistles, children playing, babies crying, heels walking up stairs, glasses clinking in a bar? Is the soundtrack urban or rural? Is it naturalistic or not? If it includes sounds which cannot be reproduced naturally – for example, the roar of a dinosaur or the buzz of a spaceship – then how have these sounds been achieved? Are they sounds which have been used for different purposes, such as the hiss of electronic doors or air brakes to create spaceship noises, or have they been deliberately crafted using technology? What effect does the soundtrack have upon the finished film? Does it heighten tension, or create a feeling of familiarity or unease?

Consider whether the music is part of the action and is therefore **diegetic**, i.e. it can be heard by the characters and is part of the visualised scene, or **non-diegetic** music which is laid over the top of the action and cannot be heard by the characters? For example, if the characters in a scene go to a party, can they hear the music which is playing or has the music simply been added for the edification of the audience? In a montage sequence is the character dancing around to music which they can hear or are they simply being shown in a variety of short cuts and edits while an unrelated song plays over the top? Is the music being produced by a character in the film playing an instrument, or performing a song in a nightclub, for example, as in *Cabaret* (1972)? Or is the music a mixture of both as in *Billy Elliott* (2000), where Billy has a series of songs which he dances to played out on a cassette tape, as well as other songs which are overlaid over extensive montage sequences? The choice of songs can again offer an insight into character – mournful songs for break-ups and deaths, upbeat songs for dance routines and happy occasions. Certain films craft their own musical scores and assign particular music to individual characters; the storm-trooper march from *Star Wars* (1977) is always associated with the sinister Darth Vader, while in the Indiana Jones films, the non-diegetic music triumphantly rings out to accompany particularly daring behaviour by the eponymous hero, notably when he is escaping the clutches of his Nazi pursuers. In *Jaws* (1975) the two-note repetition used to signal the shark's approach proved to be both menacing and effective in harnessing suspense. The association of a particular character with a specific piece of music is a **leitmotif** and the leitmotif in *Jaws* signals danger and the approach of the shark. This particular leitmotif is so widely known and has been so much cited, referenced and parodied that the two-note musical cue will inevitably remind audiences of the original film, as well as the dangers associated with it. When analysing musical cues, leitmotifs, recorded music and original scores, you need to think about how all the different audio effects are layered on top of each other, what the dominant effect is, and how the aural elements are working together or against one another.

For example, in Francis Ford Coppola's *Apocalypse Now* (1979), one of the most significant elements is the music; Wagner's 'Ride of the Valkyries' blasting out as the helicopters move towards the village is one of most disturbing and spectacular scenes within the film. In this particular scene the music and the sound of rotor blades spinning, close ups of anxious faces, the script with Robert Duvall's Kilgore delivering the chilling line, 'I love the smell of napalm in the morning' as well as the spectacular visuals of the helicopters riding through the sky and the following attack on the village, all work together to heighten the tension and deliver an explosive cinematic scene.

Costume

If the film is set in the past, we need to consider if the costumes are evoking that particular historical period or are they deliberately anachronistic? Are modern touches being used to make a deliberate point about history, narrative, character or modernity, or is the film simply using costumes to signify 'the past' rather than indicate a particular period? If the film is set in the modern period then we should consider if the clothes are practical or comfortable, whether they are flashy or demure. What colour palette is being used in the costumes of individual characters? In *Cat on a Hot Tin Roof* (1958), Elizabeth Taylor principally wears white to draw attention to the whiteness of her skin, the redness of her lips, her black hair and dazzling blue eyes. She also wears a tight red belt for the first sequences in the film to draw the spectator's attention to her small waist and to indicate her sexuality and allure. Throughout the film she wears form-fitting costumes to draw deliberate attention to her figure; everything fits close to the skin and draws attention to her waist and bust. The attention given to Maggie's clothes is further enhanced by the fact that in two separate scenes she is shown in a state of undress. The viewer is placed in the position of voyeur and encouraged to look upon the character, both dressed and undressed. Taylor's costumes also act as a counterpoint to the clothes worn by the other female characters. Maggie's shrill and avaricious sister-in-law Blanche wears nondescript maternity wear which is unflattering in both cut and colour, while her mother-in-law is presented in over-trimmed clothes and with over-dyed hair (see fig. 4).

4 A partially clothed Elizabeth Taylor as voluptuous and sensual Maggie in *Cat on a Hot Tin Roof* (1958)

In *Far from Heaven* (2002), the colours within the settings and location and of the clothes are some of the standout aspects of the film. In her role as housewife Cathy, red-haired Julianne Moore wears 1950s dresses with wide skirts in deep reds and greens. These costumes help to establish the period in which the film is set and offer an element of authenticity in their attention to detail. Period detail can be easily achieved through costume, but costume and dress can also reveal a great deal about character, including hints as to sexual orientation, wealth, background and social status. The wealthy, effeminate and waspish Cecil in *A Room with a View* (1985) is always immaculately dressed. His clothes fit him perfectly and offer an image of the perfect gentleman that contrasts with the scruffiness of George or Freddy. From Cecil's clothes it is clear he is well born and wealthy, yet the stiffness of his posture, his affected way of speaking and his use of both cane and lorgnette all combine to suggest a prudishness, a fact which the audience (and Lucy) come to realise as the film unfolds.

Costumes always need to be considered in terms of how they work with the other textures and colours within the set. For example, a lavish MGM musical such as *Seven Brides for Seven Brothers* (1954) places great emphasis on colour, and yet the set itself is drab and generic, offering an easily identifiable but non-arresting visual impression of pioneer life. Interior shots are composed mainly of dark and light brown shades with an emphasis on simple wooden lines, while the outside shots are similarly rustic. The vivid colour within the film comes from the costumes worn by the characters; the coloured shirts worn by the brothers of the title which present bold blocks of deep colour and the full-skirted gingham check and pastel dresses of their girls which complement them. These costumes perform two distinct functions: one is to distinguish between the seven different brothers and their girls, the other is to focus upon the characters and their movements, particularly during the athletic and exuberant extended dance sequences. In order to make these dance sequences as vibrant as possible, the background sets are deliberately crafted to create a dull aesthetic and not to draw attention away from the characters. These costumes also work with the hair and makeup; the girls are clear complexioned and rosy cheeked with shiny hair and ringlets, while the men are healthy complexioned with rich auburn hair which appears bright and burnished in the lavish Technicolor print.

Costume can also be used to contrast with other filmic elements. Think of the visual image of the beautiful film star Lina Lamont in *Singin' in the Rain* (1952), and how this perfection is deliberately shattered when she speaks. Her squeaky vocals act as an obvious comedic counterpoint to her exquisitely costumed image, once again drawing attention to the way in which different filmic elements work together or against one another.

Performance style

Acting and style of performance is an important element of film analysis. Early film and classical Hollywood in particular is infused with melodrama. This is unsurprising considering cinema's emergence from the world of the theatre. Melodrama and over-the top delivery was the *style du jour* of silent cinema and continued well into the 1940s and 1950s, but now such stylised delivery is usually only used within individual films for a particular effect – for example, for characters to show 'bad acting' or to draw attention to the artificiality or theatricality of an individual character or performance. Melodramatic performance style can make films from the 1930s and 1940s appear unbearably stilted to modern audiences. The doomed romance between Trevor Howard and Celia Johnson which forms the basis of the narrative in *Brief Encounter* (1945) and the 'received pronunciation' accents of both stars are both evidence of the film's roots in 1940s Britain. In this period such accents and melodramatic delivery were the accepted norm in British cinema as well as being important indicators of class and identity (see fig. 5).

Melodramatic performance and accentless delivery was challenged by the new waves of the 1950s and 1960s, and within Hollywood was supplanted by naturalism in the late 1960s and early 1970s. Much has

5 Celia Johnson (Laura Jesson) and Trevor Howard (Alec Harvey) as the doomed would-be-lovers of *Brief Encounter* (1945), a melodrama for post-war Britain

been made of the style of modern actors and the adherence of many actors like Al Pacino, Robert De Niro and Marlon Brando to 'method' acting which draws on the emotions of the character to help develop performance. Other actors such as Daniel Day Lewis and Val Kilmer prepare for roles by living the lives of their characters in order to lend an authenticity to their performances. In order to analyse performance, different aspects of performance style need to be considered, including gestures, tone of voice, stance, movement, facial expressions and interaction with other characters. All of these distinct elements create a performance, but a great deal of performance is a response: the nervous traits or reactions of one character may occur in deliberate and specific response to the actions of another character.

Specific performance styles can also be ascribed to individual actors – Olivier was known for his theatrical delivery, Bogart for his scratchy voice and world-weary air, Marilyn Monroe for her breathy earnestness and Jack Nicolson for his saturnine grin and drawl. Performance can also be linked to different genres. For example, the trembling lip, the wide eyes, the ready screams are the instantly recognisable performed characteristics of a female victim in a horror film, while the swaggering posture with legs wide apart and a rolling gait, combined with a drawling voice are the hallmarks of the film cowboy. This performance 'shorthand' can help to define characters immediately, but how are these visual cues situated within the broader film? Are they accompanied by sound or costume to indicate their morality, background, future intentions or their purpose within the film? And how can we understand how these different elements come to work together?

ELEMENTS WORKING TOGETHER

When all of these different elements have been explored separately, it becomes easier to understand how they work together. Film production is always a team effort and the varying degrees of influence and importance of key members of the crew and cast can be critical in determining the look and sound of the finished film. It is popular to ascribe all creative control to the director of the film, but when the visuals are so distinctive, or the performances so iconic or the set design, costumes or music so creative, the impact of more than one person needs to be acknowledged. It is also the case that not everyone will have been equal on a film: the costumes in a fantasy film may take centre stage, but are they enhanced or obscured by the lighting or the way in which they are worn by the actor? The film may be an adaptation of a famous play, but has the screenwriter reformulated it to offer an entirely new interpretation or have the cast delivered a series of performances which far outweigh the strength of the original material? We can see the individual elements of filmmaking jostling for attention in the finished film. Filmmaker Derek Jarman spoke about the director being a 'ringmaster' and for him the challenge was to ensure that all the individual elements complemented each other and that creativity was allowed to flourish on his set. Other directors such as David Lean have a reputation for being autocratic and demanding the final say in every aspect of the film's production and post-production. Within television, the most powerful person involved in a project is usually the producer rather than the director, who may have been brought in to direct a single episode and have very little influence on the series or programme as a whole. Every film and every programme is different and any analysis must take the specifics of the filmed material into consideration.

Case study:
28 Days Later (2002)

When thinking about how the different elements work together, first consider what stands out in the finished film. For example, is the music or soundtrack heavily evocative? Does it point forward in the narrative or indicate character development, or is it instead discordant, signifying unease, tension or awkwardness? How does the camera move and how does this complement, enhance or act as counterpoint to the mise-en-scene? Often it is easiest to analyse this by selecting a key scene or short sequence.

An early scene in Danny Boyle's *28 Days Later* offers a good example of different visual and textual elements working together. The central protagonist Jim wakes up in a deserted hospital after an accident and starts to explore his surroundings. The previous sequences of the film have been unconnected to the character now waking up in hospital and so the audience is unaware of what will happen, who the character is and what bearing he will have on the rest of the narrative. Yet he is the focus of the scene that unfolds and the audience experience the following sequence through his eyes and, at times, from his point of view.

One of the first things to notice is the absence of sound or background music. There is nothing to be heard at the start of the scene and this draws attention to the emptiness of the world in which Jim finds himself. He emerges from the hospital and the camera tracks him through the urban landscape. Here the cinematography combines overhead shots, long shots and wide shots to convey the emptiness of the landscape. Jim is usually situated just off centre in the frame, again to emphasise the emptiness of the world around him and his relative size and insignificance. The editing is slow and precise; each shot is carefully composed to allow the viewer to assimilate something else from the landscape. As Jim walks away from the hospital, the camera starts to move, tracking him through a number of slow panning shots which accompany his hesitant progress. The setting of this scene is immediately recognisable as the heart of tourist London. The camera picks out familiar landmarks, including the London Eye, Horse Guards Parade, the Houses of Parliament and Westminster Bridge – all locations usually full of people. The eeriness and emptiness of these locations are further enhanced by other jarring visuals, including tourist merchandise littered on the ground, banknotes spilling from an untended cash machine and a London bus lying on its side, its windows shattered (see fig. 6).

6 The desolation of abandoned London in *28 Days Later* (2002) captured through cinematography, settings and colour

Director Danny Boyle directed these sequences during an early summer morning in London, which accounts for the quietness of the streets, but also the summer morning light which adds a watery thinness to the colour palette. Although shot naturally, the visuals only enhance the unnaturalness of this sequence; the setting is a place we recognise yet there are no people around, nothing is moving and nothing can be heard. The absence of dialogue reinforces the fact that there is no one to talk to, and Jim's aimless wanderings through the deserted streets captured by the moving camera only add to the sense of confusion and disorientation. The greyness of the buildings and Jim's pale green hospital scrubs are not intended to draw the viewer's attention. Occasional sharp splashes of colour challenge the dullness of the visuals and are heavy with meaning: a brightly coloured Benetton advert of broadly smiling people emphasising community and togetherness, a bright red London bus usually full of people but here lying empty and useless.

The stylistic features adopted for this scene also enhance a sense of narrative uncertainty. At this stage, nothing is explained and the absence of people and the emptiness of the landscape suggest some kind of disaster, either man-made or natural. The film was made a year after the terrorist attacks on New York and Washington; it is difficult not to think about global terrorism when watching these sequences.

In this sequence some stylistic and visual elements are more significant than others. It is hard to analyse performance style and costume because the only character we see is Jim, while his clothes are non-descript and anonymous. But these elements are being kept deliberately neutral in order to direct the viewer's attention elsewhere. They act as an important counterpoint to other distinct elements, including the camerawork, setting, colour palette and mise-en-scène. Sound, or the lack of it, is also an important element within this sequence; the silence that is only broken by a shrieking car alarm later in the scene deliberately draws attention to the questions that hang across the narrative and adds to a sense of unease. In later sequences in the film, other elements become more important, including the emergence and development of other characters, shifts within the visual style and a much broader range of locations and settings.

CONCLUSION

Identifying the individual elements that make up a film as well as exploring how they all fit together and the effect that this has is one of the key aspects of film analysis. Insights offered through visual analysis should be developed and supported by evidence gleaned from interviews and other sources. In order to find out details about the film's costumes, designs and sets, it is necessary to understand the background of those who created them and what they were trying to achieve. Has the costume designer worked on other similar films, do they have a background in art, music or theatre? What are the limitations of budget? Are the costumes designed to look a certain way under the lights or in a specific setting? Does one of the actors have a defined 'look' which needs to be accommodated? When it comes to film music, has the music been composed specifically for the film and if so by whom? If it has not been originally scored, then who has selected the music that will be included? How to find such sources and how to use them to develop your work will be explored in Chapters 7 and 8. The following chapter will build on the basics of film analysis outlined here and explore how textual analysis fits in with film historiography and the ways in which film has been written about, critiqued and discussed and how the discipline has developed.

NOTES

1   Sarah Barber and Corinna M. Penniston-Bird (eds.), *History Beyond the Text: A Student's Guide to Approaching Alternative Sources* (Abingdon: Routledge, 2009), p. 1.
2   Monaco, *How to Read a Film*, p. 33.

RECOMMENDED FURTHER READING

Bordwell, David and Thompson, Kristin, *Film Art: An Introduction* (Boston, MA, and London: McGraw-Hill, 2004).
Cook, Pam and Bernink, Mieke (eds.), *The Cinema Book*, 2nd edition (London: BFI Publishing, 1985).

Corrigan, Timothy and White, Patricia, *The Film Experience: An Introduction* (Boston, MA: Bedford/St Martin's, 2009).

Gibbs, John, *Mise-en-scene: Film Style and Interpretation* (London: Wallflower Press, 2001).

Orpen, Valerie, *Film Editing: The Art of the Expressive* (London: Wallflower Press, 2003).

Monaco, James, *How to Read a Film: The World of Movies, Media and Multimedia: Language, History, Theory* (New York and Oxford: Oxford University Press, 2000).

Thompson, Kristin, *Storytelling in the New Hollywood: Understanding Classical Narrative Technique* (Cambridge, MA: Harvard University Press, 1999).

4

FILM HISTORIOGRAPHY

As with all scholarly disciplines, film has its own history and its own historiography. At key moments in the study of film, certain theories, critiques and ideas have flourished. At other moments they have been challenged or deemed unimportant while other approaches have prevailed. Certain figures loom large within the discipline, and the theories they have expounded continue to influence and shape the research carried out within it. Yet the work of Laura Mulvey, André Bazin, Andrew Sarris, Rick Altman or Peter Wollen should not be viewed in isolation. These specific interventions occurred in particular periods and this context will always shape the production and reception of these theories. For example, focus on the text has underpinned a great deal of the work in film studies, as has focus on key directors, genres and film styles and movements. In certain historical periods, developments in technology, funding and personnel have heavily influenced the 'look' and visual style of the films made and also the way in which films were critiqued and explored. But how does all this relate to broader concerns and trends within historical scholarship? And how can we explore filmic works and moving image material in a range of different ways?

INFLUENCES ON THE DISCIPLINE

Film scholarship owes a great deal to its emergence from two very different fields. The two parallel influences on film are English literature and social and cultural history, and these two disciplines have informed the development of two distinct branches of film research: respectively, film studies and cinema history. Jeffrey Richards explains:

> Film studies [is] centrally concerned with the text – with minute visual and structural analysis of various films ... with the eliciting of meanings that neither the filmmakers nor contemporary audiences and critics

would have recognised ... Cinema history has placed its highest priority on context, on the locating of films securely in the setting of their maker's attitudes, constraints and preoccupations on audience reaction and contemporary understandings.[1]

Although the validity and importance of both approaches to film are now recognised, it is important to understand how the intellectual trends and fashions of the source disciplines have influenced and continue to inform much contemporary film scholarship. Literary studies sought to explore film using its established traditions of critical and textual analysis. This approach allows for a scholarly and careful exploration of the film text, with a focus on the structure, meaning, signs, and symbolism within the text. One of the most interesting tools in film analysis is concerned with semiotics, the 'language' of film and how audiences respond to the structured and coded meanings which lie within the text. Pioneered by Christian Metz in the 1960s, such work in breaking down the filmic language and seeking to understand how meaning is communicated through visual and auditory representation can help us explore the deeper textual meanings being played out on screen.[2]

Unlike semiotics, which draws on linguistics and language, the discipline of history – along with politics, media studies and sociology – approaches film in a different way, foregrounding the importance of film as a cultural object and emphasising the importance of historical context. The importance of context is recognised specifically in terms of production and reception, including acknowledging the importance of the audience. One of the more important historical trends since the 1960s has been for 'history from below', and this fits comfortably within film history approaches. Such an approach, which moves beyond the film as the site of a director's artistic vision and positions the audiences as active participants within the text/spectator relationship, demonstrates how the study of film is constantly shifting and evolving.

These very different conceptual approaches demonstrate the potential scope for scholars to explore and examine film and moving image. Film can be imagined in many different ways: for example, as an industrial product, as the result of technological advances, as an indicator of cultural anxieties, as a crafted artistic object, as a record of popular taste and a means of understanding audiences. All of these considerations have been applied to the study of film and at different times new approaches and theories have emerged which have helped to shape the discipline. In the 1950s and 1960s enthusiastic adherence to the auteur theory focused critical attention on the work of key directors such as John Ford, Alfred Hitchcock and the newly emergent French new wave directors François Truffaut and Jean-Luc Godard. In the 1970s feminist critiques began to influence the discipline more heavily; latterly exploration of film using post-modernist approaches has been popular, while more recently there has been a preoccupation with transnational cinema and world cinema as well as increased focus on shifting patterns of viewing and consuming film.

There is a mass of published works which detail the development of specific theories of film studies and these are useful, depending on what particular topic you are exploring and what theoretical and methodological approach you will be adopting. The way in which individual conceptual approaches have been specifically used by scholars will be expanded on in Chapter 6 while Chapter 5 will suggest how you can identify a research topic and approach.

In order to help situate the theories and trends within film studies, this chapter will establish the historiography of film through four key elements; film as art, film as economics, film as social history and film as a cultural object. This is not an exploration of all the different theoretical approaches but rather a survey of the key discourses which may prove most useful when thinking about film as a source. The final section will offer a case study to indicate how the same film can be explored using a range of different approaches.

FILM AS ART

The consideration of film as art draws on ideas which link film directly to other creative arts such as photography and painting. Yet, unlike paintings, sketches or engravings, film is not a static medium. It comprises a series of moving images which together create meaning. As André Bazin noted in relation to the 'realism' and 'reality' of some cinematic forms: 'A film is always presented as a succession of fragments of imaged reality on a rectangular surface of given proportions, the ordering of the images and their duration on the screen determining its import.'[3]

In the previous chapter on film aesthetics, the different filmic elements which contribute to the look of a film were identified. Many of these are elements which are the result of creative and artistic practice, but many are also technical. This 'visual language' of filmmaking did not emerge by accident but rather was the result of a combination of artistic and technological experimentation, increased film production and the desire to please audiences with focused, easy to follow narratives. The dominant visual codes which were well understood by audiences and which still exist in much mainstream narrative cinema became firmly rooted in classical Hollywood cinema of the 1920s. Continuity editing, standard shots and camera angles, eyeline matching and adherence to the 180-degree rule all combined with plot resolution and accessible narratives to offer the spectator a visual experience which swiftly became the filmic norm and which was both easily understood and enjoyable to watch. Robert Allen and Douglas Gomery suggest that the classical Hollywood style allows for a certain 'passivity' on the part of the audience as the different filmic elements all work together so that the viewer 'attends to the story being told and not to the manner of its telling.'[4]

While this may be true, and while the classical Hollywood style of plot resolution, easily identifiable characters and a formal filmic style may draw audiences into a film, modern film spectators are highly aware of the methods and the means of filmmaking. The variety of cinematic styles and forms in evidence in modern films contributes to a detailed body of film knowledge on the part of the spectator. As James Monaco points out, the more films that people see and are exposed to, the more they begin to understand about the inherent 'language' and established structure of the medium. He contends that 'people who are highly experienced in film, highly literate visually, see more and hear more than people who seldom go to the movies'.[5]

Discussions of film as art sit uneasily within the history of early cinema. Initially, film was conceived as a technical gimmick, an experimental medium and a source of cheap entertainment best suited to travelling fairgrounds. Early short films such as those by the Lumière brothers or Georges Méliès focused on the spectacular, such as *Voyage to the Moon* (1902) with its 'special effects' and colourised hand-tinted plates, or the technological – the train arriving at the station, the out-of-control motor car. These early films were not conceived as cinematic art, but rather as cheap, commercial entertainment. In the early days of filmmaking, the dominant roles were those of the producer, distributor and camera operator. Actors were usually unpaid and the idea of a 'star' or an 'auteur director' were concepts which only emerged in later periods with the growth of studios, the development of alternative and distinctive filmmaking styles and the emergence of cinemas as fixed exhibition spaces.

One of the key theories to influence film scholarship is the **auteur theory**. First propounded in the 1950s, the auteur theory was articulated by French filmmakers to respond to and challenge the prevailing trend in French cinema which decreed that the author of the source material was the key creative talent in the filmmaking process. The auteur theory positions the director at the heart of the film and suggests that the work itself is the result of the director's own artistic and creative vision. This theory still informs a great deal of work in film today, with important contemporary directors such as Quentin Tarantino or Terrence Malick frequently being cited as auteurs.

In the 1960s, discussion of the auteur theory by scholars like Andrew Sarris focused upon the possibilities of applying auteur theory to prominent American directors, while sceptics like Peter Wollen drew attention to the limitations of a theory that ascribed artistic and creative brilliance to a single individual within a highly collaborative practice. Debates about authorship are central to discussions of filmmaking as a creative and economic practice, but the auteur theory emerged at a key moment within the history of film and can only be fully understood within this context. For example, in early cinema the power resided with the exhibitors of the films rather than with the filmmakers themselves; in 1930s Hollywood it was frequently the producers who were the mercurial powerhouses behind production and who called the shots on the film set. While these figures may have held the power in early filmmaking and within the studio-centred Hollywood, they are not usually associated with creativity and artistry.

Here the duality of film emerges clearly; films are both artistic objects and commercial entities. Considerations of 'film as art' have consistently considered the dominant authors of such films as being the directors. Occasionally the creative endeavours of others involved in the filmmaking process are identified, such as the cinematographer, lighting director or costume designer, yet even when their creative input is acknowledged, they are usually considered to be working alongside the director and their work emerges as part of the director's creative vision.

All of this has been covered in detail elsewhere, and excellent readings on auteur theory can be found in textbooks by David Bordwell and Kristin Thompson (*Film History: An Introduction*) and Pam Cook and Mieke Bernink (*The Cinema Book*), and in edited collections by Robert Stam (*Film Theory*) and Leo Braudy, Marshall Cohen and Gerald Mast (*Film Theory and Criticism*).[6] Recently, film scholarship has challenged straightforward auteristic notions of reading film and cinema and has embraced theories of authorship which allow for more nuanced considerations. Work by Andrew Spicer has highlighted the importance of the producer as a creative force within the filmmaking process, while Sue Harper has effectively explored the complex and overlapping roles of the personnel involved in the Gainsborough costume films to suggest how the 'look' of a film is a result of the compromise and creativity which emerges during the filmmaking process.[7] While it may be true that a director like Stanley Kubrick, Alfred Hitchcock or Tim Burton may be involved in all aspects of the filmmaking process, it is unrealistic to attribute the visual style, set designs, lighting, camerawork, editing and production of a film to one person and hard to establish the degree of creative and artistic competence of the director as an individual.

Text-centred approaches, which argue for the importance of film as art, usually seek to place film alongside other high culture forms such as the novel or a painting. Yet film is an economic entity as well as an art form and – much more so than in the fields of art or literature – is produced by an industry rather than a series of individuals. A novel or painting may be commissioned and the editor or gallery exhibitor may have an important input into the shape or form of the finished product, yet the execution of the product itself is the usually the result of the creative work of one person. Furthermore, the creative work is usually completed before the involvement of industrial processes. This is not the case with the commercial cinema; even auteur directors need to have a budget agreed, they need to rent studio space, have a team of workers readied – both creative and practical – and have a schedule for completion of the film in place before a single frame is shot. Of course, amateur films, self-funded projects and films made for art-house distribution buck these trends and can perhaps be subject to increased scrutiny as artistic as well as commercial entities.

Consideration of film as art and the focus on the visual within film analysis works best when combined with an exploration of context. It is important to ask how the filmmaker was given so much creative freedom for the project. Why did he or she choose to work with the same creative team, what experience did different people bring to the project, and how was it funded? It is also crucially important to consider what influenced the production and the 'look' of a particular film, specifically whether the film has emerged as part of a broader film movement.

Often particular film movements have been closely allied to political, economic, social and cultural developments. In many cases, what began as fringe movements or artistic experimentation were adopted into mainstream film practice. For example, heavily influenced by art and early experimentation with the film medium in the early years of the twentieth century, **French impressionism** incorporated trends from surrealism to create an often avant-garde film experience. Films such as *Un Chien Andalou* (1929) challenged the viewer with surreal and artistic imagery using the new film technologies to subvert narrative and present film as art. Filmmakers such as Luis Buñuel, who collaborated with Salvador Dalí on *Un Chien Andalou*, devised films deliberately to challenge bourgeois complacency through the medium of film.

By contrast, **Soviet montage** was a style of filmmaking and editing which came to prominence through the work of Russian directors Sergei Eisenstein and Dziga Vertov in the 1920s. Eisenstein created sweeping historical epics to explore and reinforce communist ideology, while Vertov preferred an observational, almost documentary-style approach to capture the everyday work and lives of the people. Although very different in their topics, scope, approach and ideology, both men shared an interest in how editing as a technical process could be used to shape the artistic cinematic form. The rhythmic editing evident in Eisenstein's *Battleship Potemkin* (1925) and Vertov's *Man with a Movie Camera* (1929) used carefully composed sequences of images to elicit responses from their viewers. When coupled with a specifically designed soundtrack, these films highlighted the fact that editing together separate sections of film could, in itself, generate meaning within the text and did not simply have to be a purely mechanical means of joining different sequences together.

In a similar way to French impressionism, **German expressionism** drew on painting and design and incorporated those disciplines' distinctive stylistic features into filmmaking. The heavily stylised expressionistic sets and deliberately distorted perspective emerged in films such as *The Cabinet of Dr Caligari* (1920) and the horror film *Nosferatu* (1922) and later made their way into aspects of mainstream cinema through F.W Murnau's *Sunrise* (1927) and Fritz Lang's *Metropolis* (1927). In the late 1920s and early 1930s, Hollywood courted Lang and Murnau and brought them to work in America. With their help, the influence of the European expressionist movement began to appear in mainstream cinema and can be seen particularly in film noir of the 1940s.

The dominant mode of filmmaking was developed in the early 1920s and solidified as Hollywood made the transition from silent cinema to sound. **Classical Hollywood narrative** refers to the focus on narrative plot resolution, conventional editing techniques, easily identifiably characters, genres and styles which combined to make this type of filmmaking the dominant model for commercial cinema for the twentieth and twenty-first centuries. Many of the tropes and styles which we take for granted in conventional filmmaking are features of classical Hollywood narrative.

Italian neo-realism emerged in Italy in the immediate post-war period and has traditionally been read as offering a commentary on the social plight of the people and the nation in this period. Although visually striking, these films often privileged emotions over stylistics and were frequently shot in location using non-professional actors to create a sense of authenticity. *Rome: Open City* (1945) by Roberto Rossellini and Vittorio De Sica's *Bicycle Thieves* (1948) address the moral and economic brutalities of life in war-torn and post-war Italy.

Italian neo-realism would in turn influence new waves of filmmaking across Europe which would come to prominence in the 1950s and 1960s. These **European new waves** emerged in a number of European countries in this period, notably France, Britain, Czechoslovakia and Poland. Directors like François Truffaut and Jean-Luc Goddard in France and Lindsay Anderson and Karel Reisz in Britain produced work to challenge many of the conventions and assumptions of Hollywood filmmaking. A focus on style and aesthetics which privileged the look of a film above the characters or narrative resolution revolutionised filmmaking and challenged many of the assumptions about the role of the film's director as a straightforward interpreter of the written word.

These distinct film movements led in turn to other movements: Hollywood drew on the new wave to incorporate stylistic features in the 1970s, German expressionism found a home within the genres of film noir and horror, while neo-realism is frequently cited, along with documentary, as one of the most important visual styles of realist filmmaking.

Film has long cultural and visual roots and the influence of many of these movements can be seen in contemporary filmmaking. Modern filmmakers and visual artists frequently cite the influence of these important film movements as points of inspiration. It is easy to see the influence of Eisenstein's famous 'Odessa steps' sequence in Brian De Palma's *The Untouchables* (1987), where he reproduces this tense and eloquent scene almost shot for shot, or to see traces of *Breathless* (1960) in Quentin Tarantino's discursive sequences in *Pulp Fiction* (1994), complete with jump cuts and distinctive camerawork.

Exploring film as art means being aware of the influence of past modes and trends within filmmaking on contemporary directors, designers and cinematographers. Yet film is also a form created and predicated on a financial model of production, distribution and exhibition. Perhaps the most effective way to explore film is to recognise that it is both an art form and a commodity and that its creative aspects and its economics need to be considered alongside one another.

FILM AS ECONOMICS

While a range of theories exist to help us understand film, many of these focus on the text of the films themselves. However, as film is a cultural product usually created for profit, the relationship between capital and culture must be duly acknowledged. Economic histories of film industries, particularly those of Hollywood, explore the development of technology, production, exhibition and distribution and provide an important backdrop to any work on industry in particular periods.

In terms of more general historical approaches, some historians have long desired to see film considered in more economic terms; in 1976 Paul Smith noted: 'Too often films have been discussed as though generated in a vacuum by the spontaneous power of individual genius: we have much on films as art, too little on films as consumption goods.'[8]

Drawing on **Marxist theory**, Raymond Williams argued that a cultural product such as film is inextricably linked to the economic base of the period which created it.[9] To do justice to these ideas and to recognise the changing position of film in an increasingly globalised world, we need to move beyond a straightforward link between the economic base of a society and the culture it produces. For example, how can we understand the production context of a film produced in Hong Kong which found success on the European art-house circuit and was finally released on DVD to great acclaim in America? How can we understand the link between the economic circumstances of its production and the film which finally emerged and was consumed enthusiastically by audiences all over the world? Do we need to consider the link between a globalised society and global culture and how this determines the success of a film in secondary markets such as DVD or the popularity of a film many years after its initial release? Only by considering the financial logic of individual film industries and the economic importance of films themselves, as well as the role played by audiences, can we start to understand fully the connections between culture and society. Understanding the financial side of filmmaking should not be limited to film production; work on exhibition, distribution, film festivals, marketing and branding can all help to illustrate parts of the industrial process of film which have often been overlooked. In recent years, more attention has been given to film distributors and exhibitors. Work like Stuart Hanson's study on spaces of exhibition in Britain draws attention to the neglected aspects of the film industry and maps cinema-going as a cultural process through exhibition spaces.[10]

Filmmaking in different periods fulfils different needs and it is difficult to consider any model of film culture which is not affected by economic considerations. Hollywood in the 1930s was badly hit by the Great Depression and many of the smaller studios folded during the economic downturn. It has been well documented that the Mae West vehicle *She Done him Wrong* (1933) saved Paramount Pictures from going bust, while the massively overblown and extravagant Elizabeth Taylor film *Cleopatra* (1963) proved both a box-office disappointment and a huge financial loss for 20th Century Fox, taking the studio to the brink of bankruptcy. These examples are drawn from different periods and reveal the impact audience choice has upon the success of individual films; they also illustrate the state of the film industry and the stability of Hollywood in different periods and how reliant individual studios were (and still are) upon the success of film as an economic product. Understanding film economics is twofold: firstly, scholars need to understand how the film was produced as part of an industry, for example as part of Hollywood in the 1940s or China in the 1980s. Secondly, we need to understand the specifics of how individual films were financed, where the money came from, what the release pattern for the film was and if the film was a national, international or global success or failure.

All national film industries are differently structured, financed and organised, and it is important to understand the financial motivations of specific film industries. The British film industry was subsidised by Hollywood for many years and despite government attempts to promote indigenous British production, Hollywood films continued to dominate at the British box office. This had been the case since the 1930s and the relationship between the British and American film industries – based largely on shared language and culture – continues to be unequal and occasionally uneasy. In France, efforts to promote and maintain French film culture have been more successful, particularly due to the strict enforcement of a government exhibition quota for French film and heavily subsidised domestic production.

Funding for smaller, non-Hollywood films often involves a complex and precarious network of finance. In 1970s Britain when investment was hard to come by, productions, including the musical *That'll Be the Day* (1973), were part-funded by investment from the music industry. As well as the absence of American finance, the 1970s financial slump in the British industry was also partly caused by the reluctance of the British government to subsidise filmmaking without the guarantee of financial returns. Work undertaken on different decades of British cinema has indicated the importance of archival research and the need to access source material from the production process or from the papers of the individual director or producer. If funding was granted by a bigger company, it will have kept its financial records and will have submitted end-of-year accounts and statements. The difficulty is often tracking down these peculiar and often difficult to access caches of information. Chapter 7 will identify a range of sources which can be used to explore film production, exhibition and distribution, and Chapter 8 will suggest how such sources can be analysed.

FILM AS SOCIAL HISTORY

Studying films – and this broad definition should encompass amateur-made films and documentary films as well as feature films and films made for television – can help us to better understand the recent past. In order to fully comprehend the possibilities of using film in this way, research should be firmly rooted in both historical practice and cultural analysis. Films never emerge in a vacuum; a range of competing factors will have informed their production at particular historical moments. Jeffrey Richards clarifies this position, stating:

> What the historian seeks in feature films is evidence of values and attitudes from the time the film was made, the explication in story

form of the contemporary ideas about the social and sexual roles of men and women, the concepts of work and leisure, class and race, peace and war.[11]

As Richards indicates, feature films are part of cultural history and can help us understand the period in which they were made, seen and reviewed.

Yet we need to be cautious. It is overzealous to posit a singular relationship between audiences and films, and the very notion of the audience as a homogeneous mass who respond to films in identical and predictable ways has been repeatedly challenged by generations of film scholars. The idea of film as a surviving 'social memory' of a particular period is an attractive one, but when looking at particular historical periods it is easy to see connections between culture and society of which contemporary audiences may have been wholly unaware. We do this with the benefit of hindsight and must never forget that contemporary perspectives may have been very different. As Raymond Williams observed, 'it is important to remember that, in judging a culture, it is not enough to concentrate on habits which coincide with those of the observer'.[12] In looking back to any historical period, we must be aware of our own interest in specific aspects of culture and how this informs our subsequent selectivity and research. If we are using films as historical sources, then we need to ask of them some standard historical questions which both evaluate the usefulness of the object and also recognise its unique qualities and characteristics. In the case of films, we need to consider production and reception. We need to ask: when was the film made, who made it, why was it made, what did it cost, who saw it, was it successful, what were the responses to the film?

Films, like other forms of culture, are historically situated. Filmmakers make films to appeal to contemporary audiences. If a filmmaker is out of touch with what appeals to audiences then that filmmaker's films are unlikely to be successful. But audiences are capricious and the recipe for film success is far from straightforward; there are many films which have possessed all the typical ingredients for success – top actors, huge budget, part of a franchise, backed by a major studio – and yet perform poorly. Studying these trends and examining the choices made by audiences allows us to draw tentative conclusions about popular taste and cinema-going in specific historical periods.

The link between films and society is an issue that has preoccupied critics and scholars since the early days of cinema. One of the first to propose a connection between feature film and the society which produced it was Siegfried Kracauer. Kracauer argued that a study of the films made in 1920s Germany under the Weimar Republic could be seen to both reflect and respond to the dark mood of the German people and anticipate the coming of fascism. This **reflectionist** approach sought to position film as a mirror of the society which made it and the visual representation of what Kracauer terms 'psychological dispositions ... those deep layers of collective mentality which extend more or less below the dimension of consciousness' which may exist within society.[13]

Yet film is *not* a mirror and cannot 'reflect' society in this straightforward way. Other visual forms such as television have a greater sense of immediacy which allows them to respond much more quickly to specific events. For example, sitcoms or series recorded on a weekly basis, comedy shows or quiz programmes recorded on the day of transmission all have an opportunity to be topical and relevant. Music also has the opportunity to respond to events quickly, with artists being able to record and then immediately release their music via radio or, more recently through digital spaces. The production process required by films actively prevents films responding quickly to current events, and yet, paradoxically, some films *can* capture the zeitgeist or tap into a prevailing cultural feeling or social mood. Just how films manage to do this is difficult to establish and often a specific film's resonance at a particular moment can usually only be identified retrospectively.

The notion of culture as something which draws on pre-existing values, ideology and established cultural meanings is particularly important in the study of film. Raymond Williams noted: 'The arts of writing and the arts of creation and performance ... are parts of the cultural process. They contribute to the effective dominant culture and are a central articulation of it. They embody residual meanings and values, not all of which are incorporated though many are.'[14]

Positioning film as part of, or oppositional to, the dominant visual culture can be seen in the work of many film scholars in their discussion of specific types of films or in studying a particular period in film history. In periods when the cinema was the leisure activity of choice and film was the dominant visual medium, it is easier to posit a strong relationship between film and cultural values and norms. But in an age of competing media forms and the decline of cinema audiences, such a straightforward cultural model is difficult to establish. When using films from different periods as sources, it is important to acknowledge the status of the industry in the period and map it alongside audience numbers. In Britain, film ceased to be the dominant leisure activity of choice in the 1950s, with the rise of television challenging the position of film as the established dominant culture.

So how can ideas of culture and film be usefully explored? Within British cinema scholarship, Andy Medhurst considers the notions of comedy as encapsulated in a series like the Carry On films and uses a specifically *national* framework which is informed by class and residual cultural values to explore the appeal and popularity of the series.[15] Peter Hutchings and others have adopted a similar approach in their discussions of horror films and the links between horror, the historical past and the established conventions of the horror film genre which sit alongside existing British preoccupations and anxieties. In genres such as horror and comedy it is easy to see the process of **affective participation** of the audience suggested by Christian Metz and how films are establishing a relationship between themselves, their content and the spectator. Metz contends that films 'release a mechanism of affective and perceptual participation in the spectator' and that this participation is specifically engendered in order to provoke a particular reaction and response from the audience.[16]

The producer of the Carry On series, Peter Rogers, commented on the films' appeal when he noted, 'the critics who dismiss carry on humour as old-fashioned do not realise that audiences like to see the laughs coming and to recognise them'.[17] Understanding how the jokes function and operate is a crucial part of understanding how and why the films appeal to the British sense of humour and, by extension, to British audiences. This link between the appeal of a cultural text and the expectations of the audience is an important one, and exploring this connection in relation to a range of texts could offer a fruitful line of inquiry for scholars seeking to use film to explore social history, societal norms and mores.

FILM AS CULTURAL OBJECT

While the recognition of feature film as a cultural object which is worthy of study has been a recent development, cultural objects have long been recognised as important in the study of social history. In 1926, Johan Huzinga described cultural history as a process which 'directs attention toward objects but ... continually turning back from those objects to the world in which they had a place'.[18]

While such an approach is not without its pitfalls – Williams warned that 'a culture can never be reduced to its artefacts while it is being lived' – historians and scholars have been increasingly drawn to approaches which seek to understand the active and complex relationship between the objects produced by a society and the society itself.[19] In the case of films, it is not simply enough to consider what films were popular and to draw a link between the narratives of popular films and broader events. It is only once the specificities of the medium and its production and reception have been acknowledged that the films themselves can be carefully related to events such as the Second World War, second wave feminism, the growth of trade unionism or increased economic prosperity.

It is also crucial to understand the relationship between films and audiences. In Britain the splitting of auditoria in the late 1970s, the establishment of multiplex cinemas in the 1980s and a new range of viewing options combined to provide a huge amount of choice for the discerning viewer. Today, cinemas are no longer the only place to watch films and a range of factors influence what people select to see, not least the films on offer, which are in turn determined by distribution and exhibition arrangements with specific cinema chains. Work undertaken on audiences not only focuses on the meanings present within the text itself, but also draws attention to the way the text/spectator relationship shifts in different periods and what film and the cinema offer to specific communities. Analysis of audience data to explore cinema-going activity firmly situates this aspect of film and cinema within the parameters of social and cultural history. Accessing such data can be difficult but attempting to retrieve information on and gain insight into the experience of contemporary audiences to help establish what audiences in different periods found appealing or satisfying fits in with broader historiographic trends, such as history from below. This focuses on the experience of those who consume film and the lived experience of 'ordinary people' rather than on the film as a solely creative product full of messages for the audience to decipher.

Popular taste is one of the most fascinating aspects within film studies but also one of the most complex. It is difficult to imagine Derek Jarman's *Sebastiane* (1975) with its Latin dialogue and homosexual love story being critically acclaimed in the 1940s, or the melodrama-infused and restrained emotion of *Brief Encounter* (1945) suddenly becoming popular in the 1990s. Films are a product of their time, and yet some remain popular and achieve a status which enshrines them as 'classics' or 'cult' films which can guarantee their enduring popularity. Some films which were unpopular upon their initial release enjoy critical acclaim in later periods; *Get Carter* (1971) was a box-office flop on its release yet enjoyed a revival in the 'lads culture' of the 1990s, frequently being cited by both critics and audiences as one of the neglected highlights of 1970s British cinema.

Basic information about the production of a film can be gleaned from contemporary articles in magazines and newspapers and can provide an interesting indication of how the film was being received. *Trainspotting* (1996) has attracted a great deal of critical attention and there are many detailed explorations of the film by academics, scholars and journalists which can help us to further understand the text and its subsequent appeal to different audiences. The film effectively captured the mood of the mid-1990s, but its success and popularity need to be understood in relation to the existing cultural values of the society which both created and consumed it.

Using this approach perhaps allows for an exploration of film as both a product of its time and also as something designed to appeal to audiences. The appeal of a text can be understood on several levels and there are a number of theories of authorship, star identification, narrative appeal, semiotics and textual analysis which can be used to explore the film's meaning. These theories and methodologies will be explored in Chapter 6.

As well as the approaches I have identified above, films can also be seen in a range of other contexts – for example, industrial, national, or technical. Mapping film history and film historiography in terms of technology can offer new ways to see the developments taking place in film aesthetics, while exploring films in terms of their industrial or national contexts can shed light on how films propagate national myths or situate discussions about national identity.

Case study:
Saturday Night and Sunday Morning (1960)

Saturday Night and Sunday Morning is one of the key films of the British new wave. As an important film within this aesthetic movement, it has been explored in a range of ways and offers an excellent example of how the same film can be analysed and positioned using all the different approaches outlined above.

Film as art

Directed by Karel Reisz and based on a novel by Alan Sillitoe, *Saturday Night and Sunday Morning* combines the new aesthetics and camerawork associated with the British new wave with a narrative for an affluent post-war generation. Aesthetically the film is distinctive and, along with other films of the new wave, it is shot in black and white. Film scholars have written extensively about the distinct aesthetic of the new wave films and have drawn attention to the way in which locations are used, notably through the use of long camera shots. Much has been made about the way in which the hand-held camera captures the interiors of pubs, factories and homes, as well as shots of the landscape of the industrial north. The lighter cameras and faster, cheaper film stock allowed for interior shooting in small spaces and allowed greater freedom for filming. These technical advances led the way for the development of a new look and enabled such films to be made at this particular moment. The new wave also drew on cinematic movements taking place across Europe, notably the emergence of the French new wave under the aegis of Godard and Truffaut. It is within this context that *Saturday Night and Sunday Morning* must be seen. The film also stands as a marker in British cinema, and its influence on the style of contemporary British cinema cannot be underestimated. It also draws on the ideologies of the **free cinema** movement of which Reisz was a founder member. The continuing influence of the British new wave and of the social realist aesthetic is evident in films as diverse as Mike Leigh's *Vera Drake* (2004) and Mark Herman's *Brassed Off* (1996).

Film as social history

Aesthetically, the film draws on older traditions in British cinema of documentary and social commentary. Dubbed 'kitchen-sink drama' or social realism for its engagement with issues and social concerns, the films of the new wave did not shy away from addressing issues which had previously been taboo subjects. *Saturday Night and Sunday Morning* deals with infidelity, adultery, unwanted pregnancy and violence in a candid and frank fashion. It eschews both melodrama and a moralising tone and in doing so ensured its appeal to a young adult audience. The film captures the concerns, anxieties and preoccupations of the post-war generation in the actions and thoughts of its aggressive and articulate anti-hero Arthur. As well as focusing on issues, the film also highlights the differences between the older, dutiful generation and the younger, more upwardly mobile at the start of the 1960s. The film sits uneasily between the conservatism of the 1950s and the exuberant hedonism of the 1960s.

Film as economics

The film was designed to appeal to young adult audiences and its aggressive anti-hero captured the frustrations and desires of this generation. Although the film was given an X certificate for exhibition in Britain, indicating that it was for adults only, the film went on to perform well at the box office. Made on a tiny budget, the film recouped its initial costs and was a financial success for both the production company Woodfall and the distributor Bryanston Films. The success of the film ensured that Woodfall could make further films in the new wave tradition, including *A Taste of Honey* (1961) and *The Loneliness of the Long Distance Runner* (1962), as well as films which were not part of the new wave such as the phenomenally successful *Tom Jones* (1963), which also starred Albert Finney, *Charge of the Light Brigade* (1968) and *Kes* (1969). All of these films added to the prestige of British cinema and ensured continued American investment for the rest of the decade.

Film as cultural object

The success of *Saturday Night and Sunday Morning* and its break with what had come before make it an important film to study. We need to explore what it was about its subject matter, the performances in the film, the way in which it is shot, framed and presented that made it so appealing to audiences. It is also important to consider the rest of the box office at the time this film was being exhibited. Were there similar films on offer to audiences, what were their narrative concerns and how popular were their stars? Did the film build on the success of the initial novel? Was it the presence of a new star in Albert Finney which added to its appeal? Was the fact that the film addressed issues of regional identity part of its success? Did it evoke a sense of belonging in its audience? Exploring the film in these terms helps us to understand its appeal at a particular historical moment and how it captured the zeitgeist of the early 1960s and how it should be explored and analysed.

CONCLUSION

In identifying the different historiographies of film and how different trends have shaped it both as a scholarly discipline and as a technical craft, this chapter has offered an insight into the shifting and often contradictory discourses which affect the way film is perceived, studied and critiqued. This exploration is intended to provide an overview, and key texts and approaches will be highlighted in the following chapters as a means of demonstrating how different approaches and methodologies suit different research questions and different research topics.

NOTES

1 Jeffrey Richards, 'Rethinking British cinema' in Justine Ashby and Andrew Higson (eds.), *British Cinema: Past and Present* (Abingdon: Routledge, 2000) p. 21.

2 Christian Metz, *Film Language: A Semiotics of the Cinema*, trans Michael Taylor, (Chicago: University of Chicago Press, 1991; originally published Oxford: Oxford University Press, 1974).

3 André Bazin, *What is Cinema?*, essays selected and trans. Hugh Gray, 2 vols (Berkeley, CA, and London: University of California Press, 2005), vol. 2, p. 31.

4 Robert C. Allen and Douglas Gomery, *Film History: Theory and Practice* (Boston, MA: McGraw-Hill, 1993), pp. 81–82.

5 Monaco, *How to Read a Film*, p. 121.

6 David Bordwell and Kristin Thompson, *Film History: An Introduction*, 3rd edition (New York: McGraw-Hill Higher Education, 2010); Pam Cook and Mieke Bernink, *The Cinema Book*, 2nd edition (London: BFI Publishing, 1999); Robert Stam (ed.), *Film Theory: An Introduction* (Malden, MA: Blackwell, 2000); Leo Braudy, Marshall Cohen and Gerald Mast (eds.), *Film Theory and Criticism: Introductory Readings*, 4th edition (New York and Oxford: Oxford University Press, 1992).

7 Andrew Spicer, 'The production line: reflections on the role of the producer in British cinema', *Journal of British Cinema and Television*, 1:1 (November 2004), 33–50; Harper, *Picturing the Past*.

8 Smith (ed.), *Film and the Historian*, p. 8.

9 Raymond Williams, *Culture and Society 1780–1950* (Harmondsworth: Penguin, Chatto & Windus, 1961).

10 Stuart Hanson, *From Silent Screen to Multi-Screen: A History of Cinema Exhibition in Britain Since 1896* (Manchester: Manchester University Press, 2007).

USING FILM AS A SOURCE

Jeffrey Richards, 'Film and TV: the moving image' in Barber and Penniston-Bird (eds.), *History Beyond the Text*, p. 76.
12 Williams, *Culture and Society 1780–1950*, p. 297.
13 Siegfried Kracauer, *From Caligari to Hitler: A Psychological Study of the German Film* (Princeton, NJ and Oxford: Princeton University Press, 2004), p. 6.
14 Raymond Williams, 'Base and superstructure in Marxist cultural theory' in Raymond Williams, *Problems in Materialism and Culture* (London: Verso Editions and NLB, 1980), p. 45.
15 Andy Medhurst, *A National Joke: Popular Comedy and English Cultural Identities* (Abingdon: Routledge, 2007).
16 Metz, *Film Language*, p. 4.
17 Peter Rogers, quoted in Sally Hibbin and Nina Hibbin, *What a Carry On: Official Carry On Movie Book* (London: Hamlyn, 1988), p. 11.
18 Johan Huizinga, 'The task of cultural history' in John Huizinga, *Men and Ideas: History, the Middle Ages and Renaissance*, trans James S. Holmes and Hans van Marle (London: Eyre and Spottiswoode, 1960), p. 65.
19 Williams, *Culture and Society 1780–1950*, p. 310.

RECOMMENDED FURTHER READING

Allen, Robert C. and Gomery, Douglas, *Film History: Theory and Practice* (Boston, MA: McGraw-Hill, 1993).
Bazin, André, *What Is Cinema?*, essays selected and trans Hugh Gray, 2 vols (Berkeley, CA, and London: University of California Press, 2005).
Bordwell, David, *On the History of Film Style* (Cambridge, MA, and London: Harvard University Press, 1997).
Ellis, Jack C., *History of Film* (Boston, MA, and London: Allyn and Bacon, 1995).
Grainge, Paul, Jancovich, Mark and Monteith, Sharon, *Film Histories: An Introduction and Reader* (Edinburgh: Edinburgh University Press, 2007).
Sedgwick, John and Pokorny, Michael (eds.), *An Economic History of Film* (London: Routledge, 2005).
Williams, Raymond, *Culture and Society 1780–1950* (Harmondsworth: Penguin; Chatto & Windus, 1961).

✤ 5 ✦

FORMULATING RESEARCH QUESTIONS

This chapter will suggest how to identify and formulate achievable research questions. It will offer advice on how to identify an approach which both engages with your own interests and acknowledges and draws on work already undertaken in the field. The research question you design is closely related to the kind of research you will be undertaking and the approach that you will follow. There are a number of ways in which you can begin to formulate your research question. One of the best ways to begin is to consider what specifically interests you. Is it a particular theory, a series of films, one film in particular or an individual director? Are you keen to explore stardom, costume, music or sound design? Do you want to use existing conceptions of genre or authorship to focus on understudied or overlooked material? In order to develop useful research questions, you need to plan your research and think about how to carry it out. The following sections identify the different parts of this process.

DEFINING YOUR INTEREST

What specifically do you want to find out? Are you interested in the production context and filmmaking process related to a specific film, or the broader economic and financial determinants of a film industry in a particular period? Do you want to find out more about how and why a film or a series of films were made in a specific period, or are you keen to explore issues of popular taste, audience response or box-office figures in relation to a particular decade or geographical location? Do you want to study the visual meanings of film, drawing on theories of semiotics, linguistics or psychoanalysis to explore a neglected body of work or to understand the way in which films contribute to or oppose the dominant culture of a given period? Is it the technology of filmmaking that interests you? Do you want to examine the technical innovation of specific periods and the impact such innovation had on filmmaking? Is there a particular technological feature such as 3D which you feel needs to be explored in relation to issues like the marketing and exhibiting of films?

All of these may be valid approaches and topics, but it is important to devise a research question which draws on your interests, is broadly achievable, recognises the potential problems within a given topic and builds on, develops or challenges work already undertaken by other researchers. While it is crucial to be inspired by your research topic, you must remain objective. A study of Wes Anderson may be driven by a genuine love of his films, but if you are unable to study the films or the techniques of the director objectively without resorting to glowing endorsements of the filmmaker and his filmmaking style, this perhaps is not the right topic to choose. Your criteria for selecting your subject should not simply be because you like them or enjoy watching them; there should be something about them which you feel deserves further research.

Whatever your chosen topic you now need to find out more about it. You may have been inspired by watching an individual film or hearing about a particular historical period in a lecture. Perhaps you are wondering about the cinema-going experience itself and how this can be studied using different films; or perhaps you are keen to examine how a certain theory of film analysis can be applied in a different way. Maybe you would like to explore a particular film genre in more detail, or to discover more about cinema in a different country in a particular era.

READING AROUND THE SUBJECT

Once you have identified your area of interest you should begin to read around the subject and see what work has already been undertaken in your chosen area. There is always a slightly different way you can approach a well-established and well-covered subject, but it is useful to be aware of what has already been written before you finalise your own research question and determine your own approach.

For example, if you are keen to focus on Alfred Hitchcock and authorship, you need to be aware of the massive amount of material which has been written on this subject and think about how your research could offer something new. Are you basing your work on a new collection of material which has just become available? Are you making a bold argument for collaborative authorship within some of Hitchcock's early films and the importance of key personnel in achieving the visual style or lighting concept? Or are you seeking to draw new conclusions from a close analysis of key films? Your research question should draw on what already exists and use this material to determine the work you will undertake. If you decide upon an approach which deliberately challenges or refutes previous scholarship then you need to have a good reason for such an approach and a specific and precise methodology.

Reading around the subject can also indicate what has not been done. It can help you to identify where the gaps are in the existing research and where the openings and spaces are for your own work. Remember, there is always something useful to be gained by looking again at original sources, even though they may have been utilised by other scholars. Researchers look for different things in sources and it is much better to explore the original sources (wherever possible) rather than depending on the work (no matter how rigorous) of other people. For example, a researcher may have looked at the personal papers of Peter Rogers held at the BFI to explore the relative costs of making the Carry On films in the 1960s and 1970s. You may be interested in looking at the same records, but in order to discover something quite different – for example, to establish how many women were employed on these films and in what capacity. A researcher in the future might look at the same material to explore how the production team responded to issues raised by the British Board of Film Censors (BBFC) and the content of the Carry On films. It may also be the case that your work can draw on newly available resources, such as the Hammer script archive which has recently been deposited at De Montfort University in Leicester, or the newly catalogued archive papers of producer Michael Klinger held at the University of the West of England in Bristol, or the emergence of archival material from the bond company Film Finances. Such resources may not have been available to earlier researchers and a collection of unstudied material will allow you to contribute something new to the existing field of work.

Think about the different topics which your research will cover and identify a series of keywords which can help you in your online and catalogue searches. Such an approach will also be a useful way to help you find crucial sources later in your research. These and other research suggestions will be covered in more detail in Chapter 7.

You can also look to the work of others to help you identify a useful approach. If, for example, the 1930s has been studied in a way which is heavily textual, maybe you can find a way to approach the decade differently, perhaps foregrounding the practices of the film industry or the impact of external organisations such as the BBFC. If industrial studies of particular decades dominate, then perhaps you could consider why the visual style and technological changes have been less studied and propose an investigation of visual style. If the decade has only been studied in terms of its most critically popular films, then perhaps a reappraisal of a range of other films made in the same period is required; such films may not have been as popular but they still emerge from the same industry and perhaps can offer a different insight into the period.

As well as identifying the range of theoretical approaches that have been used to study the topic you are interested in, you should also consider *why* these approaches have been used. Some decades, periods and bodies of films have richer material pertaining to them than others. You should be careful not to design an approach that depends heavily on sources which do not exist. For example, devising a study of audience response to films made in the 1970s which draws heavily on the Mass-Observation material would effectively mirror an approach undertaken for earlier decades in British cinema. However, while Mass-Observation data is incredibly rich for the 1930s and 1940s, it does not exist for the 1970s and so an approach designed in this way would be seriously flawed. Similarly, if you wanted to study the government's involvement in the film industry in the 1990s, you would struggle to access official paperwork for this period as it is not due to become available to the public until the year 2020. Later chapters in this work will indicate what resources exist and how these can be utilised, but it is useful to bear potential resources in mind when devising a research question.

You should also consider *why* earlier scholars have set about their research in the way that they have. Was their research informed by a new trend in film scholarship, such as semiotics or feminist film theory? Or does the research aim to readdress a particular body of work from a different critical standpoint: for example, to assess British heritage films from a transnational perspective, as Andrew Higson has done in his latest work?[1] Is the research part of a wider study – does it coincide with the release of new source material, the conclusion of a funded academic project or government papers recently made available under the 30-year rule?[2]

Once you have read around the topic and explored the written work of other scholars, you should consider how you will use the visual material which relates to your topic. The choices you make about the way in which film material will be used can also help to determine what methodology you follow and what specific question you devise.

HOW TO USE THE FILM MATERIAL

Film material can be used in a range of different ways depending on what you want to explore and what your approach may be. Are you going to be focusing on film and popular taste, film as a historical object, film as evidence, film and audiences, film as art or film as culture?

Are you interested in using newsreel film to explore a particular historical period? Would you want to use a series of films to explore popular taste in the 1960s or 1980s? Perhaps you are keen to study filmic issues of representation of gender, race or class, for example. Maybe you want to examine how representations of particular issues, such as disability, promiscuity or poverty are presented through film in different historical periods.

Will you be exploring film using close textual analysis, or focusing on key scenes or thematic preoccupations within case study films? You should consider if you will be tracing the same tropes and themes across different film work. Is the film itself the object of study or it is simply one of a range of sources which will be analysed alongside literature, music or television programmes?

Are you looking to use film to help you understand a historical period in more detail, for example to study films of the early 1950s to better understand post-war attitudes to class, or to consider the films of the 1980s as a response to Thatcherism? Are you only interested in film which had a theatrical release or are you also going to be studying amateur filmmaking practices, avant-garde films, filmmaking co-operatives, films made for television and films made by organisations like the GPO or the Ministry of Information? Your definition of 'film' could include newsreel footage screened in cinemas, or later included in television documentaries or broadcast news reports. All of this visual material can be of great interest to the researcher, but you need to think carefully about what questions you want to ask of the material and how you will use it.

As well as considering how *you* will use the film material, you again need to think about what approaches have been favoured by other scholars. Often the key films from specific decades have been heavily examined. For example the 1970s in Britain has consistently been studied through films like *A Clockwork Orange* (1971), *Get Carter* (1971) and the James Bond films, as if these few texts are entirely representative of filmmaking in the period. Similarly, in America in the late 1960s, the films which are consistently analysed are high-quality independent productions such as *Bonnie and Clyde* (1967), *Easy Rider* (1969) and *The Graduate* (1967). This is not to say that these films are unimportant, but rather that continued focus on a few seminal texts can often restrict and limit understanding. As any historian knows, interpreting the broadest possible range of sources is far more effective in shedding light on a historical period than focusing on a single source. The study of franchises and series such as Hammer horror or the Pink Panther comedies focus the attention on the popular and successful but can be restrictive in understanding the period as a whole.

Considering a period in terms of what is popular can be a risky approach, partly because determining what audiences watched and responded to can be hard to establish. While it may be possible to establish what was the most popular or most viewed film in a specific year, it does not follow that everyone who saw this film, watched nothing else in this particular year. Some cinema-goers may have chosen to see both *Twilight* and *Iron Man* in 2008, while others may have selected *Sex and the City* over *The Boy in the Striped Pyjamas*. Some people may have seen all of these films at the cinema in this year, while others would have been restricted by age categories and might have seen *Wall-E* instead. The relative popularity of these films does not necessarily help us understand precisely who went to see them, how they responded to them and the age and gender composition of that individual viewing audience. As Robert Allen and Douglas Gomery point out, the notion of a film audience is simply 'an abstraction generated by the researcher', and audiences are constantly being 'constituted, dissolved and reconstituted with each film-going experience'.[3]

As researchers, we must also be aware that in selecting films as objects of study we run the risk of abstracting these objects from their wider context. When determining a research question and identifying a range of material to study, you must be aware of issues of selectivity, subjectivity and bias. Will you look at a range of films from the same genre? Or films released in the same year? How will you determine which films you will study and which you will not? Do you have access to all the films you need for your research? If you are studying the 1930s, it may be easy to get hold of the lavish Wilcox-Neagle productions and the Hitchcock classics, but what about the musicals of George Formby, Gracie Fields or Jessie Matthews? It may not be possible to track down particular titles which feature heavily in contemporaneous accounts and lists of box-office data.

Are you focusing on 'quality' productions or those deemed to be culturally important or valuable by previous scholars? Have the films you have chosen been accorded cult status in recent years, are they held up by critics and scholars as high points of cinematic art or practice, or has their quality or importance only been recognised in recent years? Or are you focusing on low-brow genres such as horror or sex comedy and, if so, what do you hope to gain from your study of these genre-specific films?

SELECTING YOUR FILM AND NON-FILM MATERIAL

Once you have determined how you will use your films within your research you will need to start compiling a list of additional sources relevant to your topic and approach. This would usually fall into two categories – visual material and written sources – yet could also include material which can be accessed online, as well as DVD extra features, commentaries and documentary material. The types of material available for research will be discussed in Chapters 7 and 8, but this section is concerned with how you determine what will be most useful for your research.

If we consider the films themselves to be the key sources, then researchers are in an enviable position in terms of availability of resources. Unlike medieval manuscripts or rare books, mainstream and theatrically released films are readily available, and accessing them seldom requires a trip to a library or an archive. While you may find that the films you want to study are easily available, you should also remember that issues of access and availability can determine and influence research. For example, getting hold of a copy of *Blade Runner* (1982) is pretty straightforward, but what specifically have you managed to access? Are you examining the version that was released into cinemas, the first DVD edition, the version which is screened on television, or the more recently released director's cut? While these may appear to be minor issues, it is crucial to remember that contemporary audiences may have seen a different version of the feature film, probably one without extra features and one which may have been cut for theatrical release. This is particularly important when conducting detailed textual analysis and also when considering the audience response to a specific film.

Generally, American, British and European feature films are widely available, and even if they are 'art house' or documentary they can usually be tracked down. Gaining access to copies of rarer films or programmes can be tricky, but advice on how to do this will be offered in the later chapter on resources. When it comes to identifying your objects of study, it is important to note that studying some periods is definitely easier than studying others. Many films from the silent period no longer exist and what does exist has been heavily studied, perhaps in order to compensate for what is missing. As with any sources, you need to consider what has been kept and whether the object which remains is 'typical' or completely atypical. Questioning the resources which exist is a crucial part of research; you must consider if a film has been retained because of its status – for example, is it an early film from a famous director, or is it the only surviving fragment of a much larger collection which can only be understood as part of that collection? Perhaps an individual film is seen as the highlight of a European director's work and so has been released on DVD, while other lesser works remain undigitised and unavailable. Or what of the vast amount of moving image content which does not fall into the commercial or feature-film bracket and so may be difficult to find? Amateur film collections offer a massive amount of scope for the researcher but accessing collections of amateur footage can be time consuming and difficult. They may also be preserved in a format which depends on the researcher having access to the original materials within an archive. It is unlikely that they can be removed and studied at length and there may be issues of copyright and access. All of these considerations will inform how you use the available material and what kind of research question you devise.

DEVISING A RESEARCH QUESTION

The advice offered above may seem very general and so the following case studies are examples of how you can begin defining your own research question and what you need to do in order to begin work. This approach can be applied to any question or topic and the principles indicated below – such as identifying possible sources, reading around a subject and acquiring as much readily information as possible before finalising a question – will benefit any piece of work in this area, from an essay to a dissertation.

Case study:
The Lady Vanishes (Alfred Hitchcock, 1938)

Your initial interest in a topic may stem from an interest in a single film, in this case, *The Lady Vanishes* (1938). So how can you devise a research question or find a specific topic based upon this film?

Defining an initial interest

Firstly, consider why you find the film interesting. Perhaps you found the narrative particularly absorbing or entertaining, or the characters appealed to you. Are there elements of performance style or mise-en-scene which you want to focus on? Or are you interested in the specific thematic preoccupations of British 'eccentricity' or European politics? Maybe you are interested in finding out more about the production of the film, the response of audiences and why it emerged at a particular historical moment.

Any of these issues would be valid ones for research and it is important to remember that you do not need to have a finalised question when you begin your research. It is better to have a clear focus and yet be flexible enough in your approach to incorporate whatever you may discover during the research process. This way, your research findings can inform your final question, rather than you having to fit your research into the limits of your previously defined question.

After considering this film in detail, perhaps you have decided to explore how the film presents the British characters and how these representations resonated with British audiences. However, at this early stage of research it is wise to be cautious and not to make assertions which cannot be supported or set out to 'prove' something which cannot be proven. It is far better for the research to be undertaken with an open mind. To this end a *possible* research question can be a useful way to begin.

Possible research question: How did Hitchcock's *The Lady Vanishes* (1938) explore and represent aspects of British national identity in the 1930s?

You have identified your particular interest in the topic and now need to start to read around the subject, to devise a methodology and consider the approach that you will use.

Approach: Film as a cultural object and as social history and close textual analysis of key scenes.

Understanding why a film emerged at a specific historical moment is crucial when using film as a source, and research which draws upon a range of material allows the film scholar to understand both the process of production and the response to the completed film. This kind of research also permits the scholar to make observations and draw conclusions from the evidence, rather than making spurious and unsubstantiated claims about 'the audience' or the general popularity of the film which cannot be established. Of course, the nature of the research carried out relates closely to what you are trying to find out. In this instance the research may cover a range of different ideas and it may be useful to think of the keywords which could be associated with your topic and question.

Research areas to be explored/keywords: National identity, audience response, 1930s, visual style, film as social and cultural comment, stereotypes, Hitchcock.

Reading around the subject

Before focusing specifically on the film itself, it is good to discover more about the period in question. In this instance the period being considered is Britain in the 1930s. To gain an understanding of this particular period and of the British film industry, as well as seeing what other films were being made in the period, a range of material should be identified such as:

Sources
Jeffrey Richards, *The Age of the Dream Palace: Cinema and Society in 1930s Britain*.
Rachael Low, *Film Making in 1930s Britain*.
Jeffrey Richards, *The Unknown 1930s: An Alternative History of the British Cinema 1929–1939*.
John Sedgewick, *Popular Filmgoing in 1930s Britain: A Choice of Pleasures*.

Robert James, *Popular Culture and Working-Class Taste in Britain 1930–39: A Round of Cheap Diversions?*

This material will provide information on the film industry in the 1930s and what other films were being made as well as how the 1930s is being explored by film scholars. It would be useful to know what films were popular in 1938 and how these other films dealt with issues of national identity and presented the British character. This kind of information could be gathered from the pages of film industry publications such as *Kinematograph Weekly* and movie fan magazines such as *Picturegoer*, which features interviews with stars as well as reviews and features.

It is easy for modern audiences to view *The Lady Vanishes* as an exploration of the director's concerns about the imminent war in Europe, yet it is far harder to find concrete evidence that Hitchcock was actively preoccupied with European politics and decided to use his film project to explore British isolationism and the political alliances forming in Europe. Discussing the cultural importance of the film, finding contemporary reviews that reflect on the content of the film and the intentions of the director, the performances of the stars, and the reactions of audiences can all provide an understanding of how the film was received upon its release in 1938. As with any film, the possibilities for research into production and reception are extensive, and this question fits in well with an approach that explores film as a cultural object and as part of social history. Sarah Street's *British Cinema in Documents* offers a useful model for this kind of approach.[4]

If the focus of the research is to understand the popularity of a film and its possible thematic resonance with audiences, then responses from contemporary audiences, box-office data and cinema ledgers are essential sources. Is it possible to find out more information about where the film was shown? Where did it have its premiere, how long did it run? Was it distributed in America or throughout Europe? Did the film encounter any problems with the British Board of Film Censors and can these records be accessed? Did the film's stars – Margaret Lockwood and Michael Redgrave– give interviews at the time of the film's release discussing the filmmaking process? Have they subsequently published autobiographies where they talk about the making of the film and working with Hitchcock?

To understand why the film was made in 1937, further contextual research could be carried out, perhaps using newspapers, magazines and radio programmes to explore how national identity was being configured for consumption. As part of this research it would be important to establish what characteristics were being presented in this historical period as being quintessentially 'British' and if any of these qualities can be seen in the representation of the characters within the film. Again, secondary material can be of use here, including publications which deal specifically with the issue of national identity such as Jeffrey Richards' *Films and British National Identity: From Dickens to Dad's Army*.

In addition, it might be useful to look at more general material on the 1930s such as Juliet Gardiner's *The Thirties: An Intimate History of Britain*. Such background research could be developed by considering a range of newspapers to see how events in Europe were being reported by the general press. Are all the headlines about war and politics? What other stories are making the front pages? Other contextual information should also be considered; specifically, who was in government at the time and what was the government's attitude towards the film industry?

Another strand of this research could be to consider the importance of the film's director. There are a number of useful biographies of Hitchcock which may cover his response to the film and how he reflected on it at later stages in his career:

Sources

Mark Glancy, *The 39 Steps* (British Film Guides).
Barry Keith Grant and Maurice Yacowar, *Hitchcock's British Films*.
Tom Ryall, *Alfred Hitchcock and the British Cinema*.
Andrew Sinclair, *Masterworks of the British Cinema: Brief Encounter, Henry V, The Lady Vanishes*.
François Truffaut, *Hitchcock: A Definitive Study of Alfred Hitchcock*.
Robin Wood, *Hitchcock's Films Revisited*.

Visual sources

As well as watching *The Lady Vanishes*, it would also be helpful to study other films made in the 1930s, particular those released at the same time which may have had similarities to the film you are studying. Other films made by Hitchcock in the period should also be viewed to look for similar thematic preoccupations, while for general background other audiovisual material such as newsreel footage of events in the 1930s could provide a useful introduction to the period. It is a good idea to try and find recorded interview with members of the cast or with the director. The BBC archive has an audio recording of a programme called *Alfred Hitchcock in his Own Words*, while the television archives of BBC and ITN may provide useful interview footage with Margaret Lockwood and Michael Redgrave, and the British Pathé newsreel archive could be searched for other information relating to the stars, the director and the film.

Case study:
trade unionism on the screen

This second case study focuses on how both factual film and feature film can be used to explore an aspect of life in Britain – specifically, trade unionism. Once again the first thing you need to do is to determine your focus. Will you focus on the issue of trade unionism and how this has been represented on screen over a period of years, or are you focusing on a specific period and the range of different representations within that period?

Unlike the previous case study, which focused on how to develop a question based on a single film, this example draws on imagery and ideas which can be found in a range of filmed material: news reports, feature films, newsreels and documentaries. So you will need to consider how these individual representations are generated, in what form and in what context. Specifically, are they newsreel images with accompanying voiceover which was relayed into cinemas? Do they form part of a collection of newsreels such as British Pathé or Movietone, and does this help us to understand why they were made? Or are they television reports screened in later decades which are making use of earlier footage? Are they filmic representations and, if so, where do they emerge from – what were the preoccupations of the actors, the screenwriters, the directors, the producers? Are these fictional representations based on real events? Are they intended to be realistic or comical? Are they designed to appeal to or to challenge an audience? Can we look at the representations evident on screen and tentatively link them to broader social and political events? And what sources exist which would allow us to do this?

Are you focusing on how these images were received as well as created? If so, it will need to be made clear that audiences understand these images in different ways in different periods. Representations of trade unionism in the 1970s and 1980s at the height of public standoffs between the government and trade union factions will be very different to reportage of the General Strike of 1926 or of trade union activity in the 1950s or 1960s.

At this stage of the research, your question could remain very broad and could be, for example:

Proposed research question: Trade unionism on the screen: factual and fictional depictions of trade union activity 1950–1980

This would provide enough space to research thoroughly and explore the broad issue of trade unionism on the screen and to cover films addressing trade union activity, as well as examining newsreel footage of trade union action such as the General Strike and news coverage of strike action in the 1980s. Such an approach would allow for an initial comparison between fictional and factual representation, but could be narrowed down at a later stage of research. For example, it may be that you identify a shorter period of time to explore in detail, or even to isolate a few key years to compare and contrast different representations from different years.

Approach: Issues of representation and the use of both factual and fictional film as a means of understanding depictions of trade unionism, film as culture, film as evidence, film as social history, visual representation.

Research areas to be explored/keywords: National identity, representation, factual film and bias, objectivity, newsreels, audience response, film as social and cultural comment.

Reading around the subject

Once again this will depend on the particular focus of the work, but a general introduction to the subject could include reading up on trade unionism in Britain in the twentieth century. Useful work could include:

Sources:
John McIlroy, Nina Fishman and Alan Campbell, *The High Tide of British Trade Unionism?: Trade Unions and Industrial Politics, 1964–79.*

Henry Pelling, *A History of British Trade Unionism.*

You could even trace the discourse about trade union activity through articles and editorials in different newspapers to explore a range of attitudes. Reading such detailed background accounts of the broad topic will also help to indicate a way for you to narrow down your focus. For example, it may be that after reading about British trade unionism, you want to further explore the clashes between Thatcher and the unions – specifically the miners in the 1980s and how this was explored within a range of film material. You may have been intrigued about references to Thatcherism and union activity in films such as *Brassed Off* (1996) or *Billy Elliot* (2000).

If this is the case, you will need to consider both the period in which the films are set and the period in which they were made. Why did the film industry in Britain not address union activity in the 1980s, but rather waited until the following decade to do so? Was this to do with structures of funding or the way in which the industry was organised? Work by John Hill and Robert Murphy which addresses both the films and the production context of the British film industry in the 1990s will provide a useful introduction to the preoccupations of the industry in this period and valuable information on how these two films were funded. Lester D. Friedman's *Fires Were Started: British Cinema and Thatcherism* focuses on the impact of this political ideology on the film industry in Britain and how filmmakers challenged or absorbed the Thatcher legacy. As well as material which relates specifically to the film industry, you could also consider work which addresses Thatcher and the unions such as David Marsh's *The New Politics of British Trade Unionism: Union Power and the Thatcher Legacy.*

Another strand of the preliminary research could be to consider how feature films tackle the issue of union activity through close textual analysis and explorations of content and theme. Within these films, are union activists and the cause which they stand for presented sympathetically or are they played for laughs? What does this then suggest about the topic of unionism in Britain at this time? Is it possible to trace the roots of this kind of comedy to similar films in British cinema – for example, the representations of the union representatives in *I'm Alright Jack* (1959) and *Carry On at Your Convenience* (1971)? You should also draw on work which focuses on the link between film and society, including Anthony Aldgate and Jeffrey Richards' *Best of British*, which includes a chapter on *I'm Alright Jack*.

If you want to explore newsreel representation you should make sure that you understand how and why newsreel films were made and why they were exhibited in cinemas. Luke McKernan's *Yesterday's News: The British Cinema Newsreel Reader* is a good introduction and will help identify what collections of visual material will be most useful and how this material can be analysed.

Visual sources

As well as the feature films already mentioned, you should consider other forms of visual material which can help to explore the issue of trade unionism on the screen. Television programmes from the BBC and ITN archives about the miners' strike and previous government responses to trade union activity could offer a useful range of material, while newsreel footage could again offer an insight into attitudes towards strike activity and union activity in the early part of the twentieth century. Once you have identified what your interest is you could also track down interview material with people such as Arthur Scargill, Margaret Thatcher, James Callaghan and Harold Wilson, who will have given interviews to articulate their views on strikers and union activists.

CONCLUSION

The two case studies outlined above indicate how you can set about devising a research question. Now that you have drawn up a question or series of questions, read around the subject, identified your sources and devised an approach, you should consider the methodology of your research – how you are going to carry it out. Issues of methodology will be discussed in the next chapter, but it is important for methodology to be closely allied to approach. As will be shown in the following chapter, a methodology can be devised once the preliminary work is undertaken and a clearer picture of your specific question begins to emerge.

NOTES

1   Higson, *Film England*.
2   As of 2013, the thirty-year rule is being progressively scaled down to a twenty-year rule, with the process intended to be complete by 2022. See www.nationalarchives.gov.uk/about/20-year-rule.htm (accessed 8 December 2014).

3   Allen and Gomery, *Film History*, p. 156.
4   Sarah Street, *British Cinema in Documents* (London: Routledge, 2000).

RECOMMENDED FURTHER READING

Allen, Robert C. and Gomery, Douglas, *Film History: Theory and Practice* (Boston, MA: McGraw-Hill, 1993).

Chapman, James, Glancy, Mark and Harper, Sue, *The New Film History: Sources, Methods, Approaches* (New York and Basingstoke: Palgrave Macmillan, 2007).

Ó Dochartaigh, Niall, *Internet Research Skills: How to Do your Literature Search and Find Research Information Online* (Los Angeles: Sage, 2007).

Robson, Colin, *How to Do a Research Project: A Guide for Undergraduate Students* (Oxford: Blackwell, 2007).

Walliman, Nicholas, *Your Research Project: A Step-by-Step Guide for the First-time Researcher* (London: Sage, 2000).

Wheatley, Helen, *Re-viewing Television History: Critical Issues in Television Historiography* (London: I.B. Tauris, 2007).

✻ 6 ✻

THEORY AND METHODOLOGY

The previous chapter has indicated how to identify a topic, a research question and an approach. This chapter will demonstrate how you marry that approach to an appropriate methodology and critical framework. It will also survey a selection of important theories in film studies that can be used to frame work in the field.

Some approaches to studying film privilege the archive, others the text, others advocate a conceptual or theoretical framework. Certain approaches favour certain topics but, as with all scholarship, reasons for considering specific theoretical approaches must be clearly delineated. The work of theorists and philosophers who have written on film such as Walter Benjamin or André Bazin can be useful in highlighting ways in which to consider film as an art form. Others, including Raymond Williams, address the cultural specificity of film, while scholars like Christian Metz consider the codes and language of cinema to formulate a structuralist approach. The methodology and theory you decide to use will depend on your topic, your approach and your sources. One of the best ways to understand the links between a topic, a methodology and theoretical approach is to see how other scholars have achieved this.

When using film as a source, there is no need to reinvent the wheel. While film is not an old and firmly established discipline like history or philosophy with a canon of scholarly work dating back many hundreds of years, there is an extensive body of writing on all aspects of film. Some of this work is conceptual or theoretical, other work may be empirical. Some writings may focus on technology, economics or industry, others may focus on film texts drawn together by generic conventions, thematic similarities or historical convergence, while others still privilege a single text or present a series of 'typical' case studies. The range of approaches deployed within the broad field of film studies demonstrates the scope for the film researcher. As well as providing a selection of methodological models, much published material can help to indicate further research paths and identify established research that is in need of reappraisal.

In addition to the critical work on film, which is expanding all the time, the researcher can also benefit from the easy availability of the film resources. Unlike some aspects of social or cultural history where the historian has to imagine the events of the French Revolution or to read about them using a range of primary and secondary sources, the film researcher can easily access film material from earlier historical periods. While films can be 'read' and interpreted in different ways, their form and structure is recorded and preserved. Although the experience of the spectator and the means of viewing may be different, the body of the film will generally be the same as that released into cinemas. In this way, the film scholar has a rare advantage in this almost unique access to the historical objects of study.

This chapter will highlight a range of work in the field, suggesting how and why the work was undertaken and how the methodology, theoretical or conceptual approach adopted can be utilised in your own further research.

WHAT IS A METHODOLOGY?

A methodology is the approach that you decide to adopt. Unlike the more formalised methodologies found in the sciences, the study of film does not foreground a single methodological approach. As film developed as a discipline, different methodologies also developed; some adhered to processes of film critique and textual analysis, while some espoused archival work and the importance of historical and social context. As shown in Chapter 4, the development of film as a discipline has been heavily shaped by different trends, methodologies and approaches. Movements such as Italian neo-realism or the British new wave emerged at key historical moments, and the films themselves were critiqued and theorised in specific ways which can be linked to the prevailing critical and methodological fashions. When beginning your own analysis you should be aware of the link between film movements and the critiques which accompanied them.

For some research it is most appropriate to utilise a textual approach – for example, when considering an aspect of cinematography or analysing the visual qualities of a film. However, if your approach requires you to understand why changes in cinematography occurred in a particular period, you will need to link the technical changes identified to changes discernible within the visual style of specific films. If you are keen to explore how specific issues are represented on film, then you will need to pay attention to the context in which the films were made.

As already identified, the distinctions between different methodological approaches are not firmly fixed. Often a methodology which marries the best of both – text and context – can offer a thorough and complementary approach. A combined approach acknowledges the importance of film as a visual text and also as a cultural and historical product. It is also possible to draw on the strengths of related methodologies from the humanities and sometimes it is essential to do so. For example, if you are undertaking interviews as part of your research, the methodologies associated with gathering oral history should be incorporated into your overall methodology.

Depending on your topic and the question you have identified, your methodology should enable you to carry out the best research you can while also acknowledging the limitations of what you can realistically achieve. Your chosen methodology must provide you with a framework which complements your research questions, but which also allows you space to make new discoveries and to incorporate ideas which may fall outside the original theoretical approach. When beginning any work which uses film as a source, relevant critical theory should be considered as a useful way of thinking about your topic but should not confine or limit your work in any way. As with any scholarly work, the intention is to be deductive rather than inductive; any methodology or critical approach which is restrictive and prevents you from taking your research in a new direction or which restricts your findings in any way may not be the right approach for you. You should be prepared to adapt your methodology and approach if necessary; you can always return to your original question and approach it in a different way if you find your original methodology or approach restrictive or limiting.

A THEORETICAL APPROACH

Selecting a theoretical approach will depend on what you are setting out to explore. If your focus is fandom or audiences then your approach may be empirical, drawing on personal recollections of films and cinema-going, setting up web forums for discussion of cinema experiences, conducting one-on-one interviews or organising focus groups. If your work is historical, your approach may be revisionist or based on newly published sources. Your methodology and approach will differ depending on what you are exploring.

Sometimes identifying an approach is straightforward: using gender theory, queer theory, feminist readings or auteur theory can be useful ways of interrogating texts from a particular director, specific genre or those with a certain textual or narrative preoccupation. Structuralist or formalist approaches are often a useful way to frame work on genre cinema, such as using the work of Mikhail Bahktin or Vladimir Propp to understand further the formal and narrative characteristics of action, romantic comedy or adventure films.[1] Scholars have used Bakhtinian models to great effect to understand notions of the carnivalesque in cinema, while Propp's work on fairytales and their narrative components has encouraged scholars to think about films in a similar formalist way.

Other topics may not fit neatly into established theoretical models. You may be keen to explore issues of female authorship, focusing on a modern film director like Kathryn Bigelow, yet perhaps none of the existing theoretical work on the auteur theory fits with the research you want to carry out. If this is the case then you need to decide if the theoretical approach you have chosen is a suitable one. To help you do this, you should perhaps consider what works and what does not when trying to use auteur theory to explore Bigelow's work. For example, you may find that your question on Kathryn Bigelow is best served by using auteur theory, but you could develop this theoretical approach by pointing out the limitations of this theory when applied to the subject in question. Using the substantial body of work on authorship as a way to begin your work could help demonstrate how key ideas can be adapted for your own research needs. Of course, in order to use the theory and amend it to suit your own needs successfully, you need to understand it thoroughly and be able to explain its strengths and limitations clearly when applied to your own work. Such a clear explanation is essential and should be included in the introduction to your work. Another way of utilising an existing theory is to demonstrate how it can be adapted to suit your own needs. For example, you could use auteur theory as the basis of your analysis but apply these debates about authorship to a producer, costume designer or choreographer rather than a director. Andrew Spicer has utilised authorship theories in precisely this way to explore the idea of a creative producer rather than of a director.[2]

Perhaps your topic can best be addressed by combining a range of theoretical approaches. Work which draws on queer theory and gay representation could also adopt an approach such as semiotics to understand the ways in which gay characters are formally 'coded' on screen and the dislocations between the formal coding of characters and their visual representations. For example, Richard Dyer's work on representation has noted that 'cultural forms do not have single determinate meanings, people make sense of them in different ways, according to the cultural (including sub-cultural) codes available to them'.[3] Dyer's influential work explores screen representations of homosexuality and considers issues of semiotics, stereotypes and the dominance of certain cultural tropes.

Regardless of what theoretical frameworks you select, the most important thing to remember is to be rigorous. The decisions you make with regard to your chosen theory have to be justified; it is not enough to select a feminist approach to critique action adventure films of the 1980s: you must explain why this is the most appropriate theory for your purposes and why it is particularly useful. You also have to explain to your reader why you have chosen the films in question and married them to this particular theory. The selection of a critical approach should not simply be based upon a fondness for the individual theory, nor should it simply be 'lifted' from someone else's work and clumsily applied. For example, Laura Mulvey's work on visual pleasure and feminist readings of films was written in 1975 and related to a specific selection of films from the 1940s and 1950s. It was never intended to be generally applied to other periods and to other film types without distinction. Indeed, in Mulvey's later work she explicitly reassesses some of her earlier observations.[4]

Using an established theory to explore something new offers exciting research possibilities, but you should always be mindful of the historical specificity of the theory and the problems which may emerge when you move this theory out of its original critical context. It is important to remember that when the theories were created or first identified, they were probably not intended to be applied in rigid or fixed ways. At the same time, it is crucial to remember that not every theory or approach can be effectively applied to every research topic. When using any theory it is important to understand when it emerged, why it did and what it is being applied to; understanding the theory and its context is crucial to using it effectively in your own work.

As part of understanding how different theories emerged and how they have subsequently developed, it is important to read as much as possible around the subject. Regardless of whether your approach is based on auteur theory or feminist discourses, psychoanalysis or structuralism, you need to make sure that you do not overlook seminal work in the field or important recent publications, even if you think that it does not specifically relate to your chosen object of study. For example, a research project which looks at the aesthetic qualities of a selection of texts within a broad social realist tradition could present a methodology which focuses on the film texts themselves, but which also embraces the intricacies and complexities of historical and modern notions of 'social realism'. Failing to discuss, even briefly, the problems of definition of this term suggests that you have not fully understood the subject you are researching and have not considered important work already published in the field.

The same rigour should have been applied to your selection of source material; you should not simply have chosen to look at a selection of your favourite romantic comedies, but rather should have identified how these films can be used to explore a specific research question or topic, such as gendered representations or challenges to classical Hollywood narrative. Being objective is a crucial part of your research, and ways to achieve this objectivity will be discussed more fully in the chapter on writing up your research findings.

In the rest of this chapter, I will use existing work in the field of film studies to identify a range of methodological and theoretical approaches. The purpose here is not to privilege one approach above another or to evaluate the relative strengths and weaknesses of each approach or even of each work. Rather, the objective is to explore how such work has been carried out, what theories and methods are being utilised and if any of these frameworks could offer suitable and imitable models of research for your own work. Once again, the purpose is to consider what has already been written and to identify ways in which your own work can build on existing scholarship. Of course, it is important to recognise that the work identified here may have been carried out a number of years ago; it may have garnered wide critical acclaim within the discipline or provoked controversy. The impact of the work and subsequent changes or developments in the discourse need to be critiqued in your own research as part of a survey of existing literature, but the objective here is to focus on the methodological and theoretical approaches being used.

Finally, it should be made clear that none of the approaches identified will be without problems. These approaches are not being held up as hard and fast examples of how to do this kind of work, but rather to indicate how research in this particular area has been undertaken. It is the responsibility of the individual scholar to identify an approach which is both suitable and appropriate and this should be based on the compatibility of the methodology and the theoretical underpinning of approach to your own research questions.

Case study: audiences

As will become evident here, there are a number of different ways to approach the same subject. One of the most interesting preoccupations of recent years is a growing interest in reception and audience studies, an interest that can be mapped alongside broader historiographical trends which investigate the experience of 'ordinary people'.

A great deal of audience work focuses on small examples and case studies. The research carried out may relate to a single cinema, or even a single viewing of a specific film. A great deal of work has been undertaken by scholars such as Melvyn Stokes and Richard Maltby attempting to recover the experience of the earliest cinema-goers.[5] As with any research, often the approach and focus are defined by the material which is available. More detailed studies of audiences are made possible by researchers devising new ways to capture the audience experience. As Jackie Stacey has shown in her work on female spectatorship and Hollywood stars, gathering information from female spectators and exploring recorded responses in fan material allows for a more detailed and engaging picture of female identification with movie stars in the 1940s and 1950s to emerge. Stacey drew heavily on the personal responses and recollections of women who went to the cinema during this period and placed advertisements in magazines and newspapers in order to find her research subjects. Personal recollections must, of course, be treated with caution, but Stacey's methodology draws together the strengths of empirical and ethnographical work with existing discourses about female viewing and the way in which the female spectator has been critically positioned.

Within her work, Stacey demonstrates that a useful methodology can emerge which embraces both theoretical approaches to cinema and the 'female gaze' and the audience research which allows for a positioning of the active spectator. In a similar way, Robert James has used working-class 1930s audiences to explore ideas about taste, popularity and culture and how this affects the films chosen for viewing in small communities.[6] James and Stacey focus on distinct groups – James on working-class audiences and Stacey on women – and crucially both studies are historically specific. The importance of context is something emphasised by both scholars. Stacey writes persuasively: 'I would argue for the need to understand popularity and pleasure as historically located in order to theorise the full complexity of female spectators' relationships to popular culture.'[7] In adopting an approach which uses both theory and audience research, Stacey demonstrates the strength of film analysis which incorporates methods from both literature and history.

Stacey's work on audiences and spectatorship builds on other work published on film, notably feminist film theory and studies of audiences and gender. The work of scholars such as Laura Mulvey, Molly Haskell and Annette Kuhn all draw attention to gender and representation and the way in which spectators 'read' film texts. Haskell's work addresses the ways in which women have been presented on screen and relies on close textual analysis and explorations of what women as images *mean* within films.[8] Her approach is broadly historical and traces the development of female images and characterisations alongside broader social changes, changes within Hollywood itself and altered audience expectations. Mulvey uses **psychoanalytic theory** to explore both the subconscious anxieties present in films and audiences and the way in which the processes of looking and seeing are heavily gendered. Mulvey rests her ideas on a model of psychoanalysis which positions the spectator within a series of unconscious processes at work throughout the cinematic process. She suggests: 'In a world ordered by sexual imbalance, pleasure in looking has been split between active/male and passive/female ... in their traditional exhibitionist role, women are simultaneously looked at and displayed with their appearance coded for strong visual and erotic impact so that they can be said to connote *to-be-looked-at-ness.*'[9]

Annette Kuhn's exploration of feminism and cinema builds on the work undertaken by Mulvey and others but argues against ideas of the passive spectator and suggests, 'spectators, as part of their socialisation as cinema-goers build up an understanding of how to read films, so that the act of reading may eventually becomes automatic or taken for granted'.[10] Unlike Mulvey, who sees the text/spectator relationship in terms of unconscious psychoanalytical and semiotic processes, Kuhn considers that: 'Textual attributes can never be considered as operating independently of their reception, because they constitute forms of rhetoric, or ways of addressing spectators ... Meaning production in cinema in turn involves certain kinds of spectator–text relationships which are peculiar to cinema.'[11]

Kuhn's ideas and methodological approach draws more heavily on a **cultural studies model** which acknowledges the differences between spectators – particularly in terms of their class and education – and the variety of responses which individual spectators may experience when watching in the cinema. In later work on spectatorship Michelle Aaron reflects on both approaches and reminds us that Kuhn's work emerges from cultural studies and trends attendant upon it in the 1980s, while Mulvey's work grew out of 1970s feminist film theory.[12] It is also important to consider how each approach developed and what it draws upon. Theoretical models rarely emerge fully formed; usually they draw on existing ideas and are refashioned or developed in some way. As Aaron indicates, both Mulvey and Kuhn's approaches are useful, yet need to be adapted carefully for explorations of general and gendered viewing and their historical specificity particularly acknowledged.

Some explorations of audiences and their viewing pleasures are organised around generically specific films. Sue Harper's examination of the British costume film seeks to explore this particular genre of films and the cultures of production and reception which led to their creation. She identifies that these particular films not only deal with and mediate the past for audiences, but in doing so they indicate what kind of past is being preferred by those audiences, noting, 'Popular historical films were widely accepted because their audiences were able to decode the complex and sometimes inconsistent messages they bore.'[13] Also writing about costume films, Pam Cook argues that films such as the Gainsborough cycle of the 1940s refashioned notions of female desire and expectations in the post-war period through a focus on costume, narrative, character and behaviour.[14] The exploration of audiences is only part of the approach devised by both authors; Cook and Harper also engage with issues of national identity and representations of the past, as well as the intricacies of popular taste and pleasure. Harper uses the film history approach as her overriding methodology and pays due attention to the ways in which the film texts emerge from their social, cultural and economic contexts, while Cook locates her analysis of key costume drama films within broader debates about wartime and post-war national identity as well as paying specific attention to feminist discourses about gendered viewing and identity in the 1940s and 1950s.

As well as explorations of historical cinema-going activity, notably during the wartime period in Britain, recent years have seen a broadening of approaches to studying audiences. The launch of *Participations: Journal of Audience and Reception Studies* in a free online format in 2003 brought a range of new approaches into sharp relief. Contemporary scholarship explores the shifting audience/text relationships and draws on a range of examples to suggest new ways to define, research and conceptualise audiences. Matt Hills discusses the importance of textual productivity and digital fandom, while Barbara Brady offers an ethnographic exploration of cinema-going and the 'male gaze' which takes Mulvey's influential concept as a means of exploring audience responses to modern film star Mila Kunis.[15]

The different approaches to the study of audiences and the broadening of the subject to include web responses, fan forums and specifically devised ethnographic explorations of particular audiences indicate the growing interest in this area of analysis and the myriad of ways in which it can be explored. It also underlines the importance of adopting a methodological approach which best suits your own research needs. Use existing research as a base, but consider what you are exploring and what methods best suit your own approach and specific focus.

Case study:
censorship, extreme texts and regulation

This second case study addresses the different ways in which scholars have dealt with issues surrounding the regulation and censorship of film. Scholarly studies of censorship frequently draw attention to the way in which different societies regulate films and cinema, using key examples to demonstrate attitudes toward certain issues at particular historical moments. But studies of censorship also explore shifting notions of popular taste, changing cultural attitudes to taboo or extreme material and the complex relationships which exist between film and society. As well as using the films themselves to study issues of regulation, work on censorship has also used film material to explore film audiences, government involvement in the censorship process and industrial issues such as film production, exhibition and legislation.

Some of the earliest work on British film censorship by James Robertson offered a critique of the work of the BBFC, paying particular attention to standout cases and the work of the Board at different historical moments. Robertson explains how his approach

> comprises a random selection of films especially noteworthy from a censorship angle ... In most instances the detailed content has been given in the belief that censorship can be fully understood and judged only within the context of an entire film and sometimes only within the overall political and social context as well.[16]

This **case study approach** is one of the most commonly used methods of exploring and analysing films, but it privileges specific texts over others. Of course, all researchers make choices about what to include and what to exclude, yet other approaches can be used to develop this case study approach and offer different insights into this broad and complex topic. More recent work by Robertson and Anthony Aldgate has utilised a **comparative approach** to draw distinctions between the ways in which visual material is regulated in the cinema and in the theatre.[17] These accounts allow for an exploration of the texts themselves – such as *The Killing of Sister George* (1968) in both its theatrical and cinematic form – as well as the responses to these texts and what they reveal about social anxieties and norms.

As well as exploring social norms and expectations, work on censorship which emphasises context also explores industry and the shifting relationship between the BBFC and production companies and film exhibitors. Such work traces the relationship between production companies and the censorship board to explore the level of collaboration within these parts of the film industry and also sheds light on the financial implications of restricting material to particular age groups. This work, with its emphasis on industry and organisation rather than textual analysis, can be located broadly within a film history tradition and seen as a means through which a particular period of film history can be better understood. Annette Kuhn's exploration of censorship and sexuality foregrounds the importance of power relations within the censorship process, and in her study of the early days of cinematic censorship she suggests that the film industry, audiences, government and the media all have their part to play in the reinforcement of structures of censorship and regulation.[18] This methodological approach is still highly relevant and is frequently cited by scholars to call attention to the operation of the BBFC in later periods. More personal accounts offer different insights into the censorship process, such as those written by former censor John Trevelyan, providing an 'access all areas' insight into the work of the Board, but are written following Trevelyan's retirement and are very much a personal account of the Board's activities from the 1950s to the 1970s.[19] Other accounts, such as that of former Greater London Council member Enid Wistrich, shed light on the processes of local censorship and the censorship powers exercised by local authorities and city councils.[20]

As with all scholarly debates, discussions about censorship were influenced by external events, and these influenced what was studied and how it was approached. A great deal of material on film censorship was published in the 1970s – a period noted for the fraught relations between the BBFC and local and national government, as well as a whole slew of films which were seen to challenge contemporary social standards. Much of this work draws attention to the problematic cases of *A Clockwork Orange* (1971), *Straw Dogs* (1971), *The Devils* (1971) and *Last Tango in Paris* (1972) and the role played by the press, local government and pressure groups like the Festival of Light in attempting to restrict access to these films. None of these external events affects the value and importance of the scholarly work produced, but they did influence how scholars in the 1970s and 1980s wrote about the practice and politics of censorship of film and video. The shifts in the broader debate – particularly the issues highlighted in the media – also had an impact on the kind of scholarly work being undertaken, particular in recent years. One of the most recent publications in this field was published by the BBFC in collaboration with the British Film Institute (BFI) and drew on the expertise of film scholars, researchers and BBFC examiners.[21] The opening up of the BBFC archive files and the creation of numerous case studies on its website has also facilitated a shift in the way British censorship has been explored. Such an approach could provide a useful opportunity for research into contentious films and how they are handled by the organisation.

Following the 'video-nasty' debate in the early 1980s, discussions about film censorship situated the work of the BBFC and film censorship alongside broader debates about personal and social responsibility, protection of the vulnerable and general regulation of visual forms, including video and television. Publishing in 1984 at the height of the video-nasty media-based sense of outrage, Martin Barker set out to directly challenge much of the prevailing media and government rhetoric about the link between extreme videos and society, adopting a cultural studies approach.[22] Some years later, Julian Petley drew attention to the way in which government and media frequently play on social anxieties when discussing the 'power' of film and its potential to influence. Petley sees this as more than straightforwardly poor news reporting or empty political rhetoric, but instead suggests that, 'lurking behind fears about the "corruption of innocent minds" one finds time and time again, implicit or explicit, a potent strain of class dislike or fear'.[23] This link between the work of an industry organisation and the importance of broader media discourses on harm, vulnerability, influence and media effects situates both Barker's and Petley's approaches within the field of media and cultural studies. Petley himself locates these debates about extreme texts within a framework of government rulings and media debate, while at the same time arguing for a reasoned critical exploration of some significant 'nasty' titles.

Kate Egan's work adopts a similar approach, and pays due attention to context as well as to content. In doing so she suggests that the term 'video-nasty' denotes less a filmic genre and more a culturally specific term used by particular groups for a range of purposes. Egan claims that a thorough investigation of the video-nasty as a cultural product can help contribute to the burgeoning body of work which explores 'the processes, mechanisms and consequences of film censorship'.[24] Through media discourse analysis Egan indicated how cultural forms which had long been disregarded as unworthy of study could usefully be used to explore further the practices and operations of film censorship.

In recent years, a range of methodological approaches to film censorship have begun to emerge, many of them adopting a **revisionist approach** to the material presented in earlier studies, or else seeking to understanding the decision-making process at the BBFC in much more detail. The purpose of much of this work is to challenge previous assumptions made about film censorship and the BBFC. Petley's recent work focuses on the anomalies inherent in the current system of censorship and seeks to explain the reason for these anomalies, the workings of the censorship process and how and why the current censorship system continues to exist for film and videos in Britain.[25] Other approaches draw on the paper archive at the BBFC, but also incorporate elements of textual and media analysis into a critique of BBFC policy. Recent approaches have been both historical and revisionist and focus on the shifting power relationships between the censorship Board, the government and the film industry in a specific historical period. Although adopting a methodology which owes a great deal to the work of Robertson and the importance of context, such work explores the workings of the organisation through a broad and diverse range of film examples rather than a selection of individual case studies.

A recent series of publications focuses on some of the most contentious and controversial film texts released in Britain, including titles on *Straw Dogs*, *A Clockwork Orange* and *Henry: Portrait of a Serial Killer* (1990). As well as focusing in detail on the content that makes the individual films so contentious, each volume in the series explores production history, critical reception, marketing and legacy as a means of further understanding the relationship between these films and audiences. Such an approach combines close textual analysis with media discourse analysis to explore issues of popular taste, changing social standards and permissions, fluctuating boundaries and taboo behaviours. These shifting social and cultural standards are being explored using films as cultural indicators of changing social norms and ideals.

The final strand of work on censorship and the work of the BBFC is specially commissioned work on audiences. Drawing on a range of social science and media methodologies, work such as the 2007 exploration by Martin Barker *et al.* on sexual violence in films, explores how audiences respond to such material. As the authors explain:

> This research was grounded broadly within the cultural studies tradition for investigating and understanding audience responses. That tradition emphasises that real audiences are always located socially and historically, and the ways in which they respond to mediated images and narratives will inevitably relate to their sense of self and of their place in their world.[26]

This case study of approaches to contentious material and censorship indicates the variety of methodological approaches which can be utilised when exploring this specific subject. Text based or archival, case study or overview, commissioned report or media discourse analysis – all of these approaches can be easily adapted for any consideration of censorship and regulation of visual material. The focus here is Britain, but these methodological approaches can be adapted to explore film censorship in other countries, or to debates about the role of government or the involvement of the media in the censorship process and the importance of audience research in the regulation of visual content.

CONCLUSION

These two very different case studies have identified how methodological, theoretical and critical approaches to the same topic differ widely. In identifying such a broad range of ideas, this chapter has highlighted the level of overlap which exists in any given topic. You may begin by researching national identity or spaces of exhibition, but may find that your work soon encompasses trends such as transnational cinema, new forms of funding or Anglo-American collaborations. Your work on theories of authorship could develop into a study of genre which pays due attention to commonalities of visual style, of production and of personnel. Similarly, what begins as an exploration of the work of Jean-Luc Godard could extend into debates about high and low culture in France, drawing on the theoretical writings of the Frankfurt School. If your work begins as the study of a film industry in a particular period, you may find that, as well as understanding the economic determinants of any given period, you are also drawing on anthropological and sociological approaches that deal with the power and structure of institutions, such as those outlined by Mary Douglas, Michel Foucault or Erving Goffman.

While identifying a theoretical or methodological framework may appear to be a complex task, this task becomes easier when you fully understand the subject you have chosen. As you read around the subject and start to identify the body of work and the key issues you wish to explore, you will begin to see what approaches have already been used. If previous scholars have all applied theories of semiotics or the writings of Deleuze to the work of a particular director, then there is probably a good reason for this choice. The more you read around a subject, the more you will start to identify that other scholars have also made choices about what approach to adopt and what theory to utilise.

Having decided upon an approach, identified a workable methodology and a relevant theoretical framework, you are now able to start to work on your source material. The following chapter identifies how you should approach a range of sources – both visual and textual – and what skills you will need in order to explore them effectively to help you further your research and your findings.

NOTES

1 Martin Flanagan, *Bakhtin and the Movies: New Ways of understanding Hollywood Film* (Basingstoke: Palgrave Macmillan, 2009); Vladimir Propp, *The Russian Folktale*, ed. and trans. Sibelan Forrester, foreword by Jack Zipes (Detroit: Wayne State University Press, 2012).

2 Spicer, 'The production line'.

3 Richard Dyer, *The Matter of Images: Essay in Representations* (London: Routledge, 1993) p. 2.

4 Laura Mulvey, 'Visual pleasure and narrative cinema', *Screen* 16:3 (1975), 6–18; Laura Mulvey, *Visual and Other Pleasures* (Basingstoke: Macmillan, 1989).

5 Melvyn Stokes and Richard Maltby (eds.), *American Movie Audiences: From the Turn of the Century to the Early Sound Era* (London: BFI Publishing, 1999).

6 Robert James, '*Kinematograph Weekly* in the 1930s: trade attitudes towards audience taste', *Journal of British Cinema and Television* 3:2 (2006), 229–243.

7 Jackie Stacey, *Stargazing: Hollywood Cinema and Female Spectatorship* (London: Routledge, 1994).

8 Molly Haskell, *From Reverence to Rape: The Treatment of Women in the Movies*, 2nd edition (Chicago: University of Chicago Press, 1987).

9 Mulvey, 'Visual pleasure and narrative cinema', 11.

10 Annette Kuhn, *Women's Pictures: Feminism and Cinema* (London: Routledge and Kegan Paul, 1982), p. 22.

11 *Ibid.*, p. 43.

12 Michelle Aaron, *Spectatorship: The Power of Looking On* (London: Wallflower Press, 2007).

13 Harper, *Picturing the Past*, pp. 1 and 4.

14 Pam Cook, *Fashioning the Nation: Costume and Identity in British Cinema* (London: BFI Publishing, 1996).

15 Matt Hills, 'Fiske's "textual productivity" and digital fandom: Web 2.0 democratization versus fan distinction?', *Participations: Journal of Audience and Perception Studies* 10:1 (May 2013), www.participations. org/Volume%2010/Issue%201/9%20Hills%2010.1.pdf (accessed 15 October 2014); Barbara Bradby, 'Our affair with Mila Kunis: a group

ethnography of cinema-going and the "male gaze"', *Participations: Journal of Audience and Perception Studies* 10:1 (May 2013), www.participations.org/Volume%2010/Issue%201/2%20Bradby10.1.pdf (accessed 14 October 2014).

16 James C. Robertson, *The Hidden Cinema: British Film Censorship in Action, 1913–1975* (London: Routledge, 1993), p. 5.

17 Anthony Aldgate and James C. Robertson, *Censorship in Theatre and Cinema* (Edinburgh: Edinburgh University Press, 2005).

18 Annette Kuhn, *Cinema, Censorship and Sexuality, 1909–25* (London: Routledge, 1988).

19 John Trevelyan, *What the Censor Saw* (London: Michael Joseph, 1973).

20 Enid Wistrich, *'I Don't Mind the Sex, it's the Violence': Film Censorship Explored* (London: Marion Boyars Publishers, 1978).

21 Ed Lamberti (ed.), *Behind the Scenes at the BBFC: Film Classification from the Silver Screen to the Digital Age* (London: BFI Publishing/Palgrave Macmillian, 2012).

22 Martin Barker (ed.), *The Video Nasties: Freedom and Censorship in the Media* (London: Pluto Press, 1984).

23 Julian Petley, 'Us and them' in Julian Petley and Martin Barker (eds.), *Ill Effects: The Media Violence Debate*, 2nd edition (London: Routledge, 2001), p. 170.

24 Kate Egan, *Trash or Treasure? Censorship and the Changing Meaning of the Video Nasty* (Manchester: Manchester University Press, 2007), p. 9.

25 Julian Petley, *Film and Video Censorship in Modern Britain* (Edinburgh: Edinburgh University Press, 2011).

26 BBFC, 'Audiences and receptions of sexual violence in contemporary cinema', BBFC, 2 October 2007, http://bbfc.co.uk/what-classification/research (accessed 14 October 2014), 1.

RECOMMENDED FURTHER READING

Braudy, Leo, Cohen, Marshall and Mast, Gerald (eds.), *Film Theory and Criticism: Introductory Readings*, 4th edition (New York and Oxford: Oxford University Press, 1992).

Colman, Felicity (ed.), *Film, Theory and Philosophy: The Key Thinkers* (Durham, NC: Acumen, 2009).

Creeber, Glen, *Tele-visions: An Introduction to Studying Television* (London: BFI Publishing, 2006).

Jancovich, Mark, Faire, Lucy and Stubbings, Sarah, *The Place of the Audience: Cultural Geographies of Film Consumption* (London: BFI Publishing, 2003).

McKernan, Luke, *Yesterday's News: The British Cinema Newsreel Reader* (London: British Universities Film and Video Council, 2002).

Nichols, Bill, *Movies and Methods: An Anthology* (Berkeley, CA, and London: University of California Press, 1976), vols 1 and 2.

Stam, Robert, *Film Theory: An Introduction* (Malden, MA: Blackwell, 2000).

⋙ 7 ⋘

RESOURCES

The previous chapters have suggested how you can select a topic, define a question and identify an approach, methodology and theoretical framework. Having decided upon a topic and an approach, you now need to think in detail about the kinds of sources you will be using. The next two chapters deal with two distinct areas of your research; this chapter highlights the types of sources which exist and how they can be accessed while Chapter 8 identifies the specific research skills you will need to effectively use these resources.

This may seem to be a very detailed way of identifying a selection of research material. However, it is intended to highlight the range of sources which exist for the study of film and the moving image and how different approaches and topics will draw on different resources. This chapter is a useful place to begin when you want to start compiling a list of sources. These sources may fall into a number of different categories: primary, secondary, archival, government, private papers, company records, books, journal articles, web archives, databases and websites. In this chapter they are grouped together under a series of headings to help you think about the different sorts of materials you may be using within your research. It is less about distinguishing between primary and secondary sources, or digital and print resources, or film journals and industry magazines but instead is a broad survey of the types of resources which exist. While the focus of this work has predominantly been on British cinema, this chapter will also include sources of information which relate more generally to the moving image. While such a survey cannot possibly hope to be comprehensive, it will include as many types of resources as possible and also indicate how different sources of material can be incorporated into your research.

Many of these sources will be key works, seminal publications or popular collections, but even surveying the broad sweep of material available is not without its problems. Books and journals may go out of print, while online archives might become unavailable. Paper or moving image archives may lose their funding and close to the public, while personal papers or gifted collections of material may be lost or withdrawn. Even films go out of circulation, and getting hold of television programmes, non-broadcast recordings or programme rushes can be challenging. While this may make research difficult, more material is coming to light and being made available all the time. As a researcher you can only use the resources that are available to you and in doing so you will make choices about what is important for your research and how you will use it. This chapter will highlight how to make best use of the materials you have access to and how to manage this aspect of the research process.

In order to carry out effective research you need to first identify what resources exist for the topic you have chosen. Are figures available to help determine what was seen and when? Do cinema ledgers or account books exist which document the various levels of success of the films in question? Can it be established how much money each film took and when it was screened? Can movie magazines or fan letters provide evidence of film popularity and audience response to particular stars? Have the personal papers of a film's star or director been deposited in a library or archive and can they be accessed?

REFERENCE WORKS

In the early stages of your research and as already indicated in the sections on 'defining your interest' and 'reading around a subject' in Chapter 5, textbooks and reference works are a good place to begin your research.

What you select to read will depend upon your focus, but remember that the more you read, the more you will understand the topic. If your focus is cinema, then general guides on cinema may be useful, but perhaps a more helpful way to think about a research question or topic is to identify a period or era. This may be a decade, or perhaps a few years, or even a film genre or movement such as the French new wave or new Hollywood. Once you have identified your period you should run some basic searches on your university or college library catalogue using the decade and period and any key terms such as 'new wave' as keywords.

Books

If your interest is in British cinema, then the following works address the various decades and are a good place to start. These secondary resources will give you a broad understanding of British cinema and film in different decades, though, of course, they all have a different specific focus.

The early days of cinema in Britain are effectively covered in Rachael Low's exceptional seven-volume series (*History of British Film*) which traces the development of film in Britain up to 1939.[1] The 1930s are also covered in work by John Sedgwick (*Popular Filmgoing*) and Jeffrey Richards (*Age of the Dream Palace*), while the 1940s are dealt with by Charles Drazin (*The Finest Years*), Robert Murphy (*Realism and Tinsel*) and Mark Glancy (*When Hollywood Loved Britain*).[2] The war years are often covered separately, and useful work includes accounts published by Anthony Aldgate and Jeffrey Richards (*Britain Can Take It*), James Chapman (*The British at War*) and Robert Murphy (*British Cinema and the Second World War*).[3] British cinema in the 1950s is the focus of work by Sue Harper and Vincent Porter (*The Decline of Deference*), while Su Holmes explores television and film (*British TV and Film Culture*).[4] Melanie Bell considers the relationship between women viewers and 1950s cinema (*Femininity in the Frame*), while Christine Geraghty (*British Cinema in the 1950s*) focuses on gender and genre.[5]

British film and cinema in the 1960s is amply covered by Danny Powell (*Studying British Cinema*) and by Robert Murphy (S*ixties British Cinema*), while journalist Alexander Walker offers his take on the films and industry in the decade (*Hollywood England*).[6] A recent surge of interest in the 1970s means that a number of studies of this often-overlooked decade now exist, notably edited collections by Paul Newland (*Don't Look Now*) and Robert Shail (*Seventies British Cinema*) and studies by Sue Harper and Justin Smith (*British Film Culture*), Sian Barber (*The British Film Industry in the 1970s*) and Paul Newland (*British Films of the 1970s*).[7] John Hill's study of British society, the British film industry and British films serves as a great introduction to the 1980s (*British Cinema in the 1980s*), while work from John Walker draws together the films of the 1970s and 1980s (*The Once and Future Film*).[8] Robert Murphy's publication on the 1990s covers this more recent decade and explores recent British hits such as *Trainspotting* (*British Cinema of the 90s*).[9]

In addition to studies that focus on particular decades, there are a number of general sources which should not be overlooked. *The British Cinema Book* by Robert Murphy is now in its third edition and should be found in the bibliography on any topic which addresses British cinema, as should Justine Ashby and Andrew Higson's *British Cinema: Past and Present* and Sarah Street's *British National Cinema*.[10] Other volumes on British cinema include work by Jim Leach (*British Film*) and Amy Sargeant (*British Cinema*).[11] Even if the period addressed by a specific work is not of particular interest for your own chosen topic, the level and detail of research make all these important sources for British cinema. Other reference works that might prove useful include Brian McFarlane's *The Encyclopaedia of British Film*, Sarah Street and Margaret Dickinson's *Cinema and State: The Film Industry and Government* and Denis Gifford's *British Film Catalogue*.[12]

There is also material which addresses specific aspects of British cinema. For example, Andrew Spicer's work on masculinity (*Typical Men*), James Chapman on history (*Past and Present*), Leon Hunt on low-brow (*British Low Culture*), Peter Hutchings on horror cinema (*Hammer and Beyond*), John Hill on the British new wave (*Sex, Class and Realism*), Claire Monk and Amy Sargeant on heritage (*British Historical Cinema*), Steve Chibnall and Robert Murphy on crime cinema (*British Crime Cinema*) and Andrew Higson on national identity (*Film England*).[13] Also useful could be Charles Barr's account of Ealing Studios (*Ealing Studios*), Sue Harper writing on women in the film industry (*Mad, Bad and Dangerous to Know*), Justin Smith on cult cinema (*Withnail and Us*), Stuart Hanson on cinema exhibition (*From Silent Screen to Multi-Screen*), Laurie Ede on set design (*British Film Design*) and Duncan Petrie on cinematography (*The British Cinematographer*).[14]

This range of secondary material on British cinema is merely a starting point. Looking at work which addresses the decade or period you want to focus on should give you some idea of the material which has been published and which you can use in your own research. You should also study the footnotes listed in such work to identify other sources which may be crucial for the study of the period in question. In particular, you should take note of journal articles published recently which address your topic of study. Many of these studies will include research on the social, cultural and political background and may draw on publications outside the field of film studies. Using material which is written from a political, historical or economic perspective will provide you with an understanding of the period as a whole and could help to point you in the right direction for further research.

This list of key resources which has been briefly compiled here for British cinema can serve as a template for other topics. Similar lists could easily be compiled for any other national cinema or indeed for television. Identifying lists of resources that relate to topics such as alternative cinema, avant-garde film or newsreels may be more complicated. As a starting point for these topics it is again useful to think about periodisation and to read about the mainstream visual culture of the period you are interested in. Although you may be interested in alternative cinema, you should still research the period in order to fully understand the context in which both mainstream filmmaking or television production and other creative practice is taking place. If you are keen to explore artists' film or avant-garde cinema then you will need to consider how such artistic practice was organised, where it was exhibited, how it was funded and who were the key players involved. Often such practice was a direct response to the perceived failures of the mainstream, and so understanding the mainstream and conventional filmmaking of the period is essential. If you are researching newsreels then you will need to understand when and where the newsreels were shown, why they were commissioned and who they were aimed at. In order to do this, you will need to explore spaces of exhibition and examine film programmes to see how cinemas fitted newsreels into their programming.

Whatever you are studying, running basic searches in library catalogues will indicate the reference books available for the topic and from here you can start to compile a list of material to read as you begin your research. Along with general texts and book-length studies, you should also be consulting the key journals in the field to identify what current research is being carried out and how this can be useful for your own research.

Journals

There are a range of journals for film that may be useful to you in your work. As well as individual journal articles which may address your research, you can also use the methodology and critical approaches outlined in journal articles as the basis of your own research. You should make full use of any footnotes and references which accompany journal articles as they may make reference to work you have not yet read. Journals will usually either be print or digital. Your university or public library may hold print copies of certain journals or may subscribe to a service which lets you access the material online. Much older publications such as film industry publication *Kinematography Weekly* (later *CinemaTV Today*) or *Picturegoer* may be available on microfilm or microfiche in your university or public library. If your library does not have access to a specific journal then you should check the holdings at your local public library and at the British Film Institute Library in London, which holds a wide range of cinema and film journals.

The kinds of journals you should consult depend on what you are researching. There are a number of ways for you to find the right journals for your subject. You should first run some basic keyword searches on the catalogue at your university library. This will give you a better idea of the kinds of publications it holds and how you can get access to them. You could also use the search engine Google Scholar, which can be accessed from the Google homepage. The search results in Google Scholar will be articles, reviews and critiques published in academic journals, and alongside the results you will be able to see if your institution holds a copy of the article or if it can be accessed online.

Finally, a number of internet sites compile useful lists of resources. For example, Film Studies for Free includes a list of accessible resources and open access journals.[15] Other useful sites include the Museum of the Moving Image website, which includes American, European and international journals in its list of resources, and *Cineaste*, which lists critical and popular publications in the field of film and cinema studies.[16]

The following academic journals are the kind of publications that may be useful for film and moving image related work:

- *Screen*
- *British Journal of Film and Television*
- *Historical Journal of Film, Radio and Television*
- *Film Quarterly*
- *Film Comment*
- *Film and History*
- *Critical Studies in Television*
- *Sight and Sound*
- *Cineaste.*

As well as academic articles, these publications will also contain critical reviews of films and reviews of recently published work within the discipline. There are also a number of journals that are published online and are free to access and fully searchable. These include: *Bright Lights, Senses of Cinema* and *Scope*.

If you are interested in a particular aspect of film studies – for example, transnational cinema, adaptation, early cinema or amateur film – there may be a specialist journal which deals with the subject. For instance, the online journal *Participations* covers audiences and audience research, while *Vertigo* specialises in independent film, video and documentary.[17] *Variety* is an essential source for the study of Hollywood, while if your topic is related to a particular national cinema, you should explore all the publications in English and in the original language of that national cinema.[18] Research in the library and online will yield a large range of resources and it is then up to you to select the most useful ones for your areas of study. Many of these journals have websites and it can be helpful to research the publications online to determine which specific publications are most useful for you.

Magazines

As well as the film and cinema journals identified above, you could consider magazines like *Empire, Picturegoer, Films and Filming* and *Total Film*. Although a very different kind of resource from academic journals, such publications can contain plenty of useful information in the form of reviews, news articles and interviews. In the heyday of cinema, publications like *Picturegoer* offer a revealing insight into the world of popular taste and are particularly useful for exploring idea of stars and stardom. By contrast, *Films and Filming* – which ran from 1954 to 1980 – has a very different tone and includes critical reviews of middle-brow cinema as well as popular film releases. At the other end of the spectrum you have industry-focused publications such as *Kinematograph Weekly*, a long-running industry publication which would morph into the more audience-focused *CinemaTV Today* in the 1970s, and which included details on films in production and more general commentary on film funding, government involvement and the work of the Cinematograph Films Council. The range of material offered by all of these publications, as well as their tone, manner of address, style, objectives and viewpoint can all be useful sources in exploring discourses about film and cinema in different historical periods. Acknowledging the different intended audiences is important, but careful analysis of the implicit and explicit discourses about popular taste offer opportunities to interrogate ideas about audiences, pleasure, taste and popularity.

For films released very recently, there may be a lack of critical scholarship, so film magazines such as *Empire* or *Total Film* can help to fill a gap. The differing cultural status and critical authority of any publication should be carefully explored before using it as a source, but the articles, reviews and critical insights as well as the way in which the material is configured for audiences make magazines about film and cinema an important and viable resource for the researcher.

Newspapers

Newspapers are also a useful resource for film studies, and you can trace debates about screen violence and film funding, access film reviews and find interviews with directors and actors through the pages of tabloid and broadsheet newspapers. Many of the British broadsheets have online archives which date back a few years, so going to the homepage of *The Times, Observer, Telegraph* or *Independent* and accessing their recent content is fairly easy. However, some of these newspapers may require you to pay a fee if you wish to explore their online archive material. More extensive archives exist for individual newspapers. A useful resource is *The Times* digital archive, which allows you free access to articles published in *The Times* from 1785 to 2006. Similarly, the *Daily Mail* Historical Archive 1896–2004 is also fully searchable. Both resources and many more like them, including recently digitised material from publications such as the BBC magazine *The Listener* and *Picture Post*, can be accessed via subscription. Subscriptions to these resources are usually managed by your university library. It may be that access to these resources is through a provider such as Cengage, JSTOR, Project Muse or LexisNexis. You should investigate what subscriptions your university and local library hold and search their websites to see what electronic resources are available to you. Your subject or faculty librarian should be able to help you access these resources and answer any queries you may have. They may also be able to apply for free trials for specific resources to help you with your research.

PRIMARY SOURCES

The primary sources which can be used in film related research are eclectic and varied. They range from the films themselves to material which dates from the production process, such as scripts, letters and memos. As already shown in the chapter on formulating a research question, gaining access to the visual material – films, television footage, amateur material – is the best way to begin your research and to become familiar with the textual and aesthetic qualities of the material.

Films and moving image

Gaining access to feature films is relatively straightforward, particularly if you are looking at films made in Hollywood or any of the other major film industries within the last seventy years. Copies of films on DVD can be easily purchased from websites, while material which has not yet been digitised can usually be sourced on second-hand VHS via websites like eBay or Amazon. However, you may face problems gaining access to films which did not have a theatrical release, avant-garde films shown as part of an exhibition or art show, silent films from the early days of cinema or rare moving image content which has not been digitised.

If you want to study this kind of material, you need to think about how you can get hold of it. There is no point constructing elaborate research questions around avant-garde film from 1960s Germany if you are unable to obtain copies of the films or to discover anything about them. It is very difficult to conduct effective research when the object of study is missing; you need to be aware of what is available and how you can access it.

As you begin your research you should start compiling a list of the visual material you want to find. If it is mainstream feature-film material a basic internet search should lead you to the resources you want. If you cannot find material, it is worth doing the following:

- **Ask your lecturer or teacher**: If your lecturer has a particular interest in your topic then he or she may have a collection of material they may be willing to share with you. If they do not hold copies they may have a good idea where you can find them.

- **Check the library**: University libraries have collections of moving image material and you may find film material which will help your research.
- **Search for it on YouTube**: If you have a clear idea of what it is you are looking for and cannot find it elsewhere, then look for it on YouTube. If the material is there, you should try and track it down to its original source; much film material is housed in official collections and once you have identified these collections you will be able to explore the material they hold.
- **Compile key data:** Find out as much as possible about the visual material you are searching for and compile key data about it. This way you will be able to search for it by year, by contributor, by title, by screening, exhibition or release date. It may be the case that it is available online or within an archive but it has been poorly curated. If this is the case then simply searching for it by title may not locate it, but perhaps it can be found through a more detailed search by date or by production company.

The following collections all hold different kinds of moving image material. This is not an exhaustive list, but rather gives you an idea of where you can begin looking for caches of material. Again, all of these archives and collections have websites, so researching them and finding out what they have online is usually the best way to begin research:

- **The British Film Institute** holds an extensive collection of film and television material which can be viewed at its London South Bank site and at five other mediatheque sites in the UK: Derby, Wrexham, Newcastle, Glasgow and Cambridge.
- **The British Universities Film and Video Council** possesses an off-air recording service and copies of television programmes, and material screened on television can be ordered from it. It also hosts a range of moving image resources many of which can be obtained for free provided your university holds the correct subscription.
- **EUscreen** is an online free-view archive of European television material which currently holds 40,000 items from broadcasters across Europe.
- **The European Film Gateway** is an online collection of film, images and texts from twenty-four film archives across Europe.
- **Film Archives UK** is an online site which brings together thirteen different regional archives holding broadcast and amateur footage.

- **The Imperial War Museums** have a substantial collection of moving image material, including propaganda films made during the First World War.
- **British Pathé** online has an extensive collection of newsreel material and archive footage.
- **Movietone** online database contains newsreels from 1929 to 1979.
- **Huntley Films Archive** holds over 45,000 films in its online database.
- **The Moving Image Archive** is a broad collection of films and broadcast television material which can be accessed online.

As well as the films themselves, visual material such as documentaries about the production of the film or television interviews with the director or cast member can also be useful resources. Some of this material can be accessed online or may be included as an extra feature on the DVD of a feature film. You should make sure that you incorporate visual sources into your list of resources and consider how best to use such material in your broader research.

In addition to visual sources, materials which relate to the production of the film, its distribution, exhibition and reception, along with any records from bodies related to the film industry, can be very useful. These records have been split into a number of different categories below.

Company records

Company reports, financial ledgers and end-of-year accounts can tell you a great deal about the industrial processes at work in the film industry. Tracking down this information can be challenging, but the material you do find may provide details about budget, marketing, profit, loss, salaries and funding choices. It is also fascinating to consider the development of individual production companies, to understand why certain projects were shelved and why others were pursued. There is an important difference between the records of a company or an organisation and the personal papers kept by an individual. Company records will include legal and financial documentation as well as information about personnel and pre- and post-production details. The key location for information on the British film industry is the library at the BFI in London.

Located on London's South Bank, the British Film Institute Library holds material relating to film production companies. The BFI is an excellent resource for both moving image material and for industrial records, critical reviews and private collections. Some of its material is part of the BFI Special Collections and you will need to make a separate appointment to access it. A search of the BFI general catalogue for 'companies' identified a wide range of material including:

- records from the London Film Company covering the years 1913–1920;
- general production and distribution company material, including brochures, marketing and publicity documents. This wide range of material dates from the earliest days of cinema through to the 1930s and relates to companies including Gaumont, Jury's Imperial Pictures, Equity British films, Keystone and Hepworth;
- annual reports from Universal Pictures Company for the years 1957–1958;
- company records from the Incorporated Association of Kinematograph Manufacturers Ltd from the 1940s and 1950s;
- company records from the British National Film League;
- extensive production and distribution material from ABC television in the 1960s;
- general company information relating to British Pathé, Anglo-Amalgamated, Associated British and Ealing;
- records and correspondence from the British and Dominions Film Corporation dated 1931–1934;
- records and end-of-year accounts from the National Film Finance Corporation (NFFC) for the years 1949–1979.

As well as records held by the BFI, individual company accounts may be contained within the personal archives of directors or producers. Michael Klinger's personal papers include the company accounts of his Swiftdown company and are held at the University of the West of England, while papers relating to Don Boyd's company Boyd's Co can be found in his papers at the University of Exeter. Understanding how the industry worked in a given decade or period is crucial when conducting film-related research. It is difficult to understand how films flop or succeed without understanding the economic and financial contexts of production, distribution and exhibition. Using the material found in collections of company and industry accounts can add depth to your research and complements approaches which seek to understand film as both a cultural and economic product.

As well as material which relates to the industrial side of filmmaking, studio papers can also include material which relates much more closely to the production of specific films. For example, the Hammer script archive has recently been deposited at De Montfort University in Leicester and offers over 240 items in its collections for scholars keen to discover more about filmmaking at the famous horror studio.

Industry papers

In addition to accounts for individual companies, financial records from funding organisations like the National Film Finance Corporation, working papers of government committees like the Cinematograph Films Council or cultural bodies like the British Film Council can also reveal how the industry operated. The accounts of these kinds of organisations may be located in the British Library or The National Archives at Kew. If they are government records they will be subject to the thirty-year rule, but if they are outside this timeframe they should be accessible.[19] Both the British Library and The National Archives have excellent search engines attached to their websites. Useful resources from these archives include letters and memos charting the development of government policy on the film industry in Britain, the establishment of co-production agreements between Britain and other countries and the use of film by organisations such as the British Council to present ideas of 'Britishness' abroad. The British Board of Film Classification now offers researchers access to its internal documents which relate to the classification of film from the earliest days of cinema to the present. Paper files relating to material released in the last twenty years are restricted, but it has an excellent website with a large number of case studies and a fully searchable database so you can establish the precise problems with recently released films. Scenario reports and reviews for films from the 1930s to the 1950s can be found in the BBFC collection at the BFI.

Records which relate to the exhibition of films in specific areas will be stored in regional or city archives. For example, data that relate to the screening of films in 1970s Portsmouth are held in the city archives for the early years of the decade and those pertaining to the end of the decade are kept in the Hampshire county archives in Winchester.

Tracking down these kinds of records may be challenging and should be undertaken when you have a clear idea of what you are looking for.

If your interest is in television, the records of the BBC are held at its written records centre in Caversham in Berkshire, while records pertaining to the Independent Television Authority (ITA) – which became the Independent Broadcasting Authority (IBA) and later the Independent Television Commission (ITC) – are held at the University of Bournemouth.

Personal papers/private collections

Tracking down archival collections, personal papers, rare visual material or company accounts often requires painstaking research. At first glance some material may not seem to be related to film at all, but it depends on your research topic and what you are trying to find out. Begin with the resources which are easiest to find. Build up your knowledge of the topic and then start to expand the list of material you want to find. Be realistic about what you can achieve: if the key material for your topic is in an archive in Los Angeles, how are you going to access it? Do you have time to visit the archive and who would pay for you to go there?

It is also important to be realistic about what you are expected to do. You will be required to undertake detailed research for your final year dissertation, MA thesis or PhD research and any other significant research project, but such intensive research involving visits to archives and accessing rare collections will probably not be required for a standard essay.

Personal papers and private collections may contain everything from personal correspondence, letters, memos, telegrams and newspaper clippings to private notes, diaries and messages. There may be detail on unrealised projects, correspondence related to casting in specific films, documents detailing any problems experienced with the film unions or with the taxman. Some personal papers contain a massive amount of material; the papers of director Joseph Losey are extensive and include paperwork which relates to aspects of his personal as well as professional life, while Derek Jarman's papers include his personal notebooks in which he sketches his design ideas for films and include detail on costumes, characters, colour and locations.

Exploring the personal papers of a director, producer, costume designer or editor can be very exciting, but locating them can be difficult. It may also be the case that the personal papers of a certain individual do not exist in a library or archive. The papers may still be in the possession of the family, or they may have been lost or destroyed. If the papers have been formally gifted to an archive or an institution then they may well be open for research and may even have been catalogued, which can help make them easier to examine. The most likely place for papers of prominent film industry individuals is either a university library or an archive such as the BFI Special Collections, the Irish Film Institute in Dublin or the National Library of Wales in Aberystwyth.

The BFI Special Collections in London has a range of personal papers, including those from Peter Rogers, John Schlesinger, Joseph Losey, David Puttnam and Michael Balcon. The extensive Stanley Kubrick papers are held at the University of the Arts in London while the papers of Lindsay Anderson are at the University of Stirling. The Bill Douglas Centre at the University of Exeter holds papers belonging to filmmakers Gavrik Losey and Don Boyd as well as those of Bill Douglas. Some papers relating to filmmaker David Lean are at the University of Reading, and the Kenneth Branagh collection is held at Queen's University in Belfast.

There are a number of very large archives in the United States where the papers of important members of the film industry are preserved. Of course, you should consider whether you are able to visit these archives before researching their holdings or planning a trip. One of the largest collections is the Margaret Herrick Library, based in California and run by the Academy of Motion Picture, Arts and Sciences. This library has over a thousand individual collections and includes the papers of Alfred Hitchcock, actors Gregory Peck and Katherine Hepburn, directors George Stevens and Hal Ashby, and many more. The University of Wisconsin-Madison holds the papers of renowned Hollywood costume designer Edith Head, actor Kirk Douglas, television host Ed Sullivan and director John Ford. The Harry Ransom Center at the University of Texas in Austin houses the papers of actor Robert De Niro and legendary showman Flo Ziegfield as well as collections relating to playwrights Eugene O'Neill, Tennessee Williams, Arthur Miller and Harold Pinter. The UCLA Film and Television Archive in California includes papers belonging to Jean Renoir, Cecil B. DeMille, Ida Lupino and Mary Pickford. It also has significant industrial holdings, including papers from Columbia Production studios.

Detailed online searching can help you to locate these personal papers. Even if such searches do not lead you directly to the papers or the archive itself, you may pick up on newspaper stories about the opening of an archive or the gifting of material by an actor or director's family and so follow the trail from there. The next chapter will offer advice and suggestions on how to go about planning a visit to an archive as well as how to sift through the material you may find.

Audience data

Recovering the experiences of audiences is notoriously difficult as sources rarely survive. However, specific caches of information do exist and can provide fascinating data on people's responses to films as well as their reasons for going to the cinema. The Mass-Observation collection at the University of Sussex is a fantastic collection of social research material gathered over a period of years and relating to all aspects of social, cultural and political life in Britain. This material can be used to explore how attitudes towards leisure, entertainment and going to the cinema changed in different periods as well as more specific information on favourite film stars and preferred films. This material is currently being digitised and so access to the resource is becoming much easier. You can always ask your library to register for a free trial in order to gain access to the material.

It is rare for data to exist for individual cinemas, but research about audiences and about cinemas can turn up in surprising places. Sometimes film production companies gathered their own data at test screenings to explore audience response to one of their films and occasionally this data surfaces in the archives of a company or an individual. The BBFC has been conducting audience research since the earliest days of cinema. As well as historical data which can be found in some of its individual film files, data about recent audience research can also be found on its website. Often such research has been carried out in collaboration with a team of researchers and they often detail the methodology they used as well as offering some analysis and conclusions from their findings.

The BFI website also hosts historical and contemporary statistics about film-going and audiences, exhibition patterns and cinema attendance. It has been collating weekly box-office reports since 2001 and also compiles exit survey data from audiences viewing a range of films. All of this data is available on the BFI website and can be a useful way to help you establish some basic facts and hard data about cinema-going and audiences.

Digital resources

In addition to all the material covered above you should also look at the vast range of digital resources which exist. Databases of digitised material, interviews conducted with industry insiders, audience data gathered for a particular area or online responses to particular films may have been part of an earlier research project. It may be that the findings of the research project are relevant to your own research and you can usually locate these findings online through careful searching. The Broadcasting, Entertainment, Cinematograph and Theatre Union (BECTU) archive at the University of East Anglia is a collection of audio interviews with members of the British film industry. In addition to directors and producers, the interviews are also with editors, continuity workers, exhibitors and technicians and they provide fascinating nuts-and-bolts detail about the workings of the film industry. Many of the interviews have been transcribed and these written transcripts are accessible online via the BECTU website. To access this material, you will need a site login, but this can be achieved fairly easily by following instructions on the webpage.

The websites of the key industry organisations should also be explored to discover what resources are available and what new initiatives are being funded. For example, the BBC archive website includes themed collections of moving image and audio material on subjects as diverse as Enid Blyton, the appeal of James Bond, Dr Who, coal mining in Britain and a collection of radio interviews with Hollywood stars, including Bette Davis, Tony Curtis and Katherine Hepburn. All of the material can be accessed freely from the website and has great potential for use as source material.

In addition to hosting its own collections of moving image and sound material, the British Universities and Video Council website includes details on projects it is involved with. Recent projects include the Channel 4 project at the University of Portsmouth, the publication of 600 films from the Technicolor cinemagazine *Roundabout* (1962–1974) in a collaboration with the BFI and the collation of news material from BBC Northern Ireland from the 1960s and 1970s in a database called Chronicle and freely accessible to all those in British universities. You should check these websites regularly and subscribe to mailing lists so that you are aware of new developments, publications and collections. As well as listings for films and upcoming events on the BFI website, their related site, Screenonline, is an online encyclopedia of British film and television, featuring hundreds of hours of film and television clips from the collections of the BFI National Archive as well as information on British directors, actors and producers.

CONCLUSION

How to use this range of material effectively will be covered in the next chapter but it is important to remember that everything included here is just a broad sweep of the material available. Many of the resources identified here relate to British film and moving image material. Television material will require a different range of sources, while a topic covering an aspect of Hollywood film or French cinema will need to draw upon other sources. But the approach identified here and the different types of sources identified should help you begin to compile your list of resources, regardless of topic.

However, you should still be considering what resources will best help you with your research and consider how to use the material you find. The following chapter will now address how you can best use these resources and how to make sure that you get the most out of a visit to an archive, how to create an online survey or conduct a research interview.

NOTES

1 Rachael Low, *The History of British Film*, 7 vols (London and New York: Routledge, 1997; originally published Allen & Unwin, 1948).

2 John Sedgwick, *Popular Filmgoing in 1930s Britain: A Choice of Pleasures* (Exeter: University of Exeter Press, 2000); Jeffrey Richards, *The Age of the Dream Palace: Cinema and Society 1930–1939* (London: Routledge and Kegan Paul, 1984); Charles Drazin, *The Finest Years: British Cinema of the 1940s* (London: I.B. Tauris, 2007); Robert Murphy, *Realism and Tinsel: Cinema and Society in Britain 1939–48*, 2nd edition (London: Routledge, 1992); Mark H. Glancy, *When Hollywood Loved Britain: The Hollywood British Film, 1939–45* (Manchester: Manchester University Press, 1999).

3 Anthony Aldgate and Jeffrey Richards, *Britain Can Take It: The British Cinema in the Second World War* (Edinburgh: Edinburgh University Press, 1994); James Chapman, *The British at War: Cinema, State and Propaganda, 1939–45* (London: I.B Tauris, 1998); Robert Murphy, *British Cinema and the Second World War* (London: Continuum, 2000).

4 Sue Harper and Vincent Porter, *British Cinema of the 1950s: The Decline of Deference* (Oxford: Oxford University Press, 2003); Su Holmes, *British*

TV and Film Culture of the 1950s: Coming to a TV Near You! (Bristol: Intellect, 2005).

5   Melanie Bell, *Femininity in the Frame: Women and 1950s British Popular Cinema* (London: I.B. Tauris, 2009); Christine Gerarghty, *British Cinema in the Fifties: Gender, Genre and the 'New Look'* (London: Routledge, 2000).

6   Danny Powell, *Studying British Cinema: The 1960s* (New York: Auteur Press, 2009); Robert Murphy, *Sixties British Cinema* (London: BFI, 2008); Alexander Walker, *Hollywood England: The British Film Industry in the 1960s*, 2nd edition (London: Harrap, 1986).

7   Newland (ed.), *Don't Look Now*; Robert Shail (ed.), *Seventies British Cinema* (London: BFI Publishing/Palgrave Macmillan, 2008); Sue Harper and Justin Smith (eds.), *British Film Culture in the 1970s: The Boundaries of Pleasure* (Edinburgh: Edinburgh University Press, 2011); Sian Barber, The *British Film Industry in the 1970s: Capital, Culture and Creativity* (Basingstoke: Palgrave Macmillan, 2013); Paul Newland, *British Films of the 1970s* (Manchester: Manchester University Press, 2013).

8   John Hill, *British Cinema in the 1980s: Issues and Themes* (Oxford: Clarendon Press, 1999); John Walker, *Once and Future Film: British Cinema in the Seventies and Eighties* (London: Methuen, 1985).

9   Robert Murphy, *British Cinema of the 90s* (London: BFI, 2000).

10 Robert Murphy, *The British Cinema Book*, 2nd edition (London: BFI Publishing, 2001); Justine Ashby and Andrew Higson (eds.), *British Cinema, Past and Present* (London: Routledge, 2000); Sarah Street, *British National Cinema* (London: Routledge: 1997).

11 Jim Leach, *British Film* (Cambridge: Cambridge University Press, 2004); Amy Sargeant, *British Cinema: A Critical History* (London: BFI Publishing, 2005).

12 Brian McFarlane, *The Encyclopaedia of British Film*, 3rd edition (London: Methuen, 2008); Margaret Dickinson and Sarah Street, *Cinema and State: The Film Industry and the British Government 1927–1984* (London: BFI Publishing, 1985); Denis Gifford, *British Film Catalogue: Fiction Film 1895–1994, Volume 1*, 3rd edition (London: Fitzroy Dearborn, 2001).

13 Andrew Spicer, *Typical Men: Representations of Masculinity in the Popular British Culture* (London: I.B. Tauris, 2001); Chapman, *Past and Present*; Leon Hunt, *British Low Culture: From Safari Suits to Sexploitation* (London: Routledge, 1998); Peter Hutchings, *Hammer and Beyond: The British Horror Film* (Manchester: Manchester University Press, 1993); John Hill, *Sex, Class and Realism: British Cinema 1956–1963* (London: BFI Publishing, 1986); Claire Monk and Amy Sargeant (eds.), *British Historical Cinema* (London: Routledge, 2002); Steve Chiball and Robert Murphy (eds.), *British Crime Cinema* (London: Routledge, 1999); Higson, *Film England*.

14 Charles Barr, *Ealing Studios* (Moffat: Cameron & Hollis, 1998); Sue

Harper, *Women in British Cinema: Mad, Bad and Dangerous to Know* (London: Continuum, 2000); Justin Smith, *Withnail and Us: Cult Films and Film Cults in British Cinema* (London: I.B. Tauris, 2010); Hanson, *From Silent Screen to Multi-Screen*; Laurie N. Ede, *British Film Design: A History* (London: I.B. Tauris, 2010); Duncan Petrie, *The British Cinematographer* (London: BFI Publishing, 1996).

15 http://filmstudiesforfree.blogspot.co.uk.
16 www.movingimagesource.us/research/guide/type/23 and www. cineaste.com/recommended_links.
17 *Participations: Journal of Audience and Perception Studies*, www.participations. org; *Vertigo*, www.closeupfilmcentre.com/vertigo_magazine.
18 *Variety*, http://variety.com.
19 As of 2013, the thirty-year rule is being progressively scaled down to a twenty-year rule, with the process intended to be completed by 2022. See www.nationalarchives.gov.uk/about/20-year-rule.htm (accessed 8 December 2014).

RECOMMENDED FURTHER READING

Burrows, Elaine *et al.* (eds.), *The British Cinema Source Book: BFI Archive Viewing Copies and Library Materials* (London: BFI Publishing, 1995).

Foster, Janet and Sheppard, Julia (eds.), *British Archives: A Guide to Archive Resources in the United Kingdom* (Basingstoke: Palgrave, 2002).

WEBSITES

BECTU: www.uea.ac.uk/film-television-media/research/research -themes/british-film-and-tv-studies/british-cinema/oral-history -project.

BFI Screenonline: www.screenonline.org.uk.

BFI Library: www.bfi.org.uk/education-research/bfi-reuben-library.

British Pathé: www.britishpathe.com.

BUFVC: www.bufvc.ac.uk.

BBC Written Archives: www.bbc.co.uk/historyofthebbc/contacts/wac.

Harry Ransom Center: www.hrc.utexas.edu/collections/film.

Margaret Herrick Library: www.oscars.org/library.

Mass-Observation: www.massobs.org.uk/index.htm.

The National Archives: www.nationalarchives.gov.uk.

UCLA Film and Television Archive: www.cinema.ucla.edu.

USING SOURCES

The previous chapter has identified the range of sources which can be useful for the study of film. This chapter will offer suggestions on how best to use these sources. As with any research, the way in which you use the material you find will depend a great deal on your topic and research question. For example, if you are keen to explore the aesthetic qualities of film in different periods, you may not give much attention to film funding. However, if you are exploring the development of an indigenous national film industry or considering why the films of the new wave emerged in France when they did, an understanding of film finance and the economics of the historical period will be relevant. You should also ensure that adequate sources exist for your research. For instance, if you are undertaking a project on audience response and want to explore contemporary and historical reactions to the same film, then you need to be able to access historical audience data and to analyse it effectively, and also find a way to elicit responses from contemporary audiences watching the same film. To do this you will need to devise a methodology that combines data gathering and analysis with a comparative historical approach.

This chapter will indicate how different kinds of sources – textual, visual, archival, financial, oral – can be used. Different skills are needed in order to use different sources effectively. You might need to know, for example, how to utilise the financial information contained in ledgers, account books or end-of-year records, or how to conduct effective media discourse analysis on newspaper articles, fan letters or film reviews. The chapter will also offer suggestions on how to go about conducting a research interview and what can be gained by using data-gathering techniques such as questionnaires and focus groups. Advice on how to analyse a film has already been covered in earlier chapters, but some suggestions will be offered to help you effectively explore and analyse a range of moving image material, from YouTube clips to newsreel footage, from television drama to filmed interviews, from experimental films to blockbuster features.

USING TEXTUAL MATERIAL

As shown in the previous chapter, secondary material such as books and journals are an excellent starting point, while magazines, newspapers, official government papers and commissioned reports can provide important contextual detail for your research topic.

Using this second group of sources requires a particular approach. It is not enough simply to look at a range of this material and use it to support your own ideas. As with all sources, you will need to consider this material in relation to its bias, nuance, subjectivity and authorship. If you are examining material from a range of different newspapers or magazines, you need to recognise and acknowledge that the material contained within these publications will be aimed at different target audiences.

Film reviews are also published in plenty of mainstream contemporary publications, and the juxtaposition of reviews alongside the articles, letters and adverts can give you an insight into both popular taste and the target audience of the particular publication, and of the particular film. If the same film or programme is reviewed in a range of publications then you should compare the language, tone and response of the reviewers. This kind of discourse analysis needs to be located within a cultural or media studies tradition and would need to take into account the political affiliation of the particular publication, current events which may be shaping the debate around a particular film or issue and something about the reviewers themselves. If it is a politician writing a column for a daily newspaper, then his or her observations on a film may be very different to that of a filmmaker being interviewed about his or her latest release or a film critic reviewing a selection of the newest releases into cinemas. Gender, age, class background, political affiliation, status and personal opinion will all be influencing factors which will shape the review or critique.

As well as considering the articles and reviews which deal with films, you should pay attention to how the publication as a whole has been put together. Are the films reviewed or discussed in keeping with the tone and style of the rest of the magazine or newspaper? Is the target audience of the publication made clear; for example, is it for teenagers or young adults, for horror or fantasy film fans? What do you know about the publication? Is it well-established or newly arrived on the scene? What are its circulation figures and what can you discover about its aims and objectives? Many publications also have websites and these may be put together in a very different way to standard print publications – for example, the adverts could be different, suggesting a different target audience to the print edition.

Official reports on the film industry, culture of broadcasting or cinema attendance produced by the government, pressure groups or industry organisations can provide you with key industry data. If the findings have been published – such as the Williams Committee findings on obscenity and film censorship – then you should be able to access them from your university library or from the BFI Library. If the reports have been commissioned by an organisation, it is worth checking to see if the findings have been published on its website. While these official reports and explorations may provide rich data, you should remember that they have been written and produced for a purpose. You need to think about who has commissioned the study, what their particular interest is and what they are trying to find out. The way in which they have carried out the research should also be considered; is it London-centric, does it draw upon a very small sample, are its findings based on other reports or studies?

VISUAL MATERIAL

Analysing a film has been covered in Chapter 3; this section will suggest some basic ways to approach and analyse different types of visual material – newsreel footage, documentary material, television items, YouTube videos, amateur footage and online collections. There is a range of different ways in which you can explore moving images, and the methodology that you adopt will recognise the unique characteristics of your source material. In order to understand your visual material you should find written material that explores that form of the medium. For example, if your focus is YouTube or online videos then work by Jean Burgess and Joshua Green will be helpful for your research.[1] If your focus is newsreels, then work by Ciara Chambers and Luke McKernan will be a good starting point.[2] Published work which analyses television material is extensive and what is useful for you will depend upon precisely what the television material is – television drama will be approached very differently to television documentary, sci-fi or fantasy programmes or news items. Although the moving image material may be different from conventional feature films, you are still using this filmed material as a source and you should still ask of it some standard research questions and utilise the approach suggested to devise a research question and formulate a methodology.

Once you have read around the specific qualities of the visual medium you can approach your sources and ask some basic questions: what is it, who made it, where can it be found, who is it intended for and why was it created? The answers to these straightforward questions will help you to establish how your source material can be understood. For example, a YouTube video posted online in 2011 will have a very different intended audience to that of an amateur film of a birthday party made in the 1940s and gifted as part of a private collection to an archive. A television documentary on disability commissioned following the 2012 London Paralympics will have a different purpose to a news item on disability claimants and may be broadcast at a different time. As with all visual material, you must think about audience but also the purpose of the material – is it intended to entertain, to educate, to provide information?

You should also consider access, transmission and broadcast. If the item has been shown on television, when was it made and broadcast? Was it transmitted live or was it pre-recorded? What does this suggest about audience and who the item is intended for? If you are looking at broadcast material, are you studying a television series and exploring how its visual style changes over the course of time? Or are you considering how the objectives of the programme shifted during the course of its broadcast run? If the item is a newsreel, when was it shown in cinemas? What is being depicted, how are the news events of the day being presented, what tone of voice is being used by the narrator or broadcaster? With historical items like this you should also consider how they can be accessed. Are they stored in an online archive and available freely or via subscription? Should they be studied as a body of work rather than as individual items? Who were they made by and what was the ethos of the company who made them?

In the modern era, a great deal of moving image material is user-generated content which can be made quickly and then posted online and seen by millions. Such material usually bypasses conventional methods of production, distribution and exhibition, and its ease of access makes it far simpler to engage instantly with it than with other, more conventional films or programmes. Yet with such a wealth of material to choose from, how do you select items for your research? Are you looking at online videos posted by the same person or those with the greatest number of views? Or are you considering a range of amateur footage from a particular year or which has been collated as a specific collection? As a researcher you should think about what makes up the body of work you will explore and how you will use it to answer your research question.

While conventional approaches to exploring setting, lighting, costume and mise-en-scene may be less than useful for analysing many of these items, all of the visual items will have been deliberately created and crafted and should be analysed visually as well as explored culturally and historically. Studies of film have developed over many years, but analysis of modern sources such as podcasts and webcasts is still developing. Using such material as source material offers exciting possibilities, but you need to approach it with care, ask relevant and pertinent questions of the material and have clear ideas of how you will use it and for what purpose.

ARCHIVAL MATERIAL

As indicated in the previous chapter, there are many different kinds of archives, all holding different types of information. You may be accessing government material, personal papers or company records. The material may be open access or restricted, it may be catalogued or un-catalogued. You may be presented with boxes of information which have been carefully catalogued and sorted by date, by film or by project, or the boxes may be full of miscellaneous paper which you will need to sift through. All archives are different, but before visiting an archive or making an appointment you should find out as much as you can from their website. You should also contact them before you visit to check their procedures, opening hours and if there is anything you need to do in advance such as providing evidence from your university about your research or programme of study, or becoming a member of the archive or organisation and paying a membership fee.

Before you visit an archive you should undertake substantial research on its catalogue, making a note of what you want to access and which specific material you want to look at. If your catalogue searches have yielded a mass of information then you will need to think about ways to refine your search. Can you limit the range of dates you are looking at; can you look at television rather than film *and* television; is it possible to focus on a particular film project or specific television programme rather than trying to cover all the output from a particular individual? You can always make follow-up visits to the archive but being focused on your immediate research needs will ensure that you get everything you need for the piece of work you are currently undertaking.

Many archives have specific rules. Copying material may not be permitted and so you should be prepared to write extensive notes. Even if copying is permitted, as is the case at The National Archives, photocopying is expensive and you should not expect to be able to copy everything. Other archives restrict the use of digital photography so copying documents in this way may not be allowed. You may be allowed to use a laptop to make notes but some archives request that you take notes in pencil rather than using pen. If you are looking at very rare material, you may be required to wear special gloves provided by the archive and to use file supports on the table to protect the material. You will usually need to provide some basic information on the topic of your research. Most archives have agreements which you are required to sign which state that you will not reproduce any of the material without their permission and that you acknowledge their ownership and copyright of the material.

Catalogued material

If the material has been catalogued then you should only be looking at material which you have requested and which is particularly pertinent to your research. Personal papers which have been catalogued will usually be organised around different film projects or in chronological order. You should also be aware of boxes which are labelled as 'miscellaneous papers' or 'correspondence', as material contained within them might also be relevant to your research. If you are exploring a box full of material relating to a particular film project, be aware of what you are looking at. Is it material related to the production or post-production of a film? Does it contain scripts, production notes, financial information, memos and letters? Take note of individual items which are interesting, but you should also look at the material as a whole. Does the correspondence suggest a tension in the film production process? Does it document arguments between the producer and director over the marketing of the finished film? Does it reveal information about cast behaviour or salaries? Can we discern where the film was being made and how much it was costing? Is there information about distribution, marketing and exhibition of the finished film?

If you are looking at catalogued material from local or national government or industry organisations, then the presentation of the material may be very different. Personal papers can contain a lot of extraneous information, whereas government and industry collections will not usually include personal letters or memorabilia but rather will comprise only the formal and official documentation and correspondence.

Any material which is used in your own research will need to be properly cited so you must make sure that you have the document information and the information which relates to the file in which it was found. For example, if you are citing the notes from a meeting between members of the government and Mary Whitehouse in 1975, you will need to reference it as fully as possible and according to the reference system you have been instructed to use. Archive material referenced in a footnote could run as follows:

Comments by Mary Whitehouse taken from meeting notes dated 5 February 1975 File HO 300/166.

The in-text citation could be:

(Mary Whitehouse, 5 February 1975)

with the full reference in the bibliography including detail on the specific Home Office file.

Government files or material accessed from any national archive will always have a specific reference number or code. The above reference – HO – indicates that the file related to work at the Home Office, while the sequence number makes it easy for anyone reading your work to follow up on your references. Referencing will depend on the referencing style favoured by your department or institution and the different forms along with the kind of information you want to include will be covered briefly in the following chapter.

Un-catalogued material

If the material you are examining has not been catalogued you will need to work through methodically. When working with material like this it is always helpful to construct a narrative of the events recorded within the documents. For example, if you are tracing a film's progress through the BBFC, then you need to be aware of any specific problems it encountered, any delays experienced in the issuing of a certificate and any bartering that went on between the Board and the production company or distributors. If the paper file is a mess it can be helpful to work through the material in chronological order to establish the sequence of events taking place.

Working with material in this way requires patience; you may not be able to find precisely what you require as key evidence may be missing. If this is the case then you must make sure that you account for these omissions and do not simply ignore them. Even if there are gaps in the archive, what remains will still be useful. If material is missing, why do you think this is? Has the material been poorly curated or stored? Has only official documentation been kept and everything else destroyed? Within the BBFC paper files, a receipt for an issuing certificate should always be present, as should formal reports from at least two BBFC examiners. Along with this official documentation there may also be letters of complaint from members of the public, memos, correspondence between the filmmakers and the Board, publicity materials for the film and sometimes press clippings. As the BBFC material is un-catalogued and the contents of the files vary widely, it is never clear what you may find. Some 1970s files contain data on audience research carried out for particular films, while others include personal correspondence from film industry luminaries such as Lindsay Anderson, Joseph Losey and Ken Russell.

If the material has not been formally catalogued then you should make sure that you cite your sources as comprehensively as possible. If, for example, you are citing work from a classification film file then your footnote could be:

Correspondence between Stephen Murphy (BBFC) and executives at Tigon Pictures dated 8 August 1972, taken from BBFC file: *Oh Calcutta!*

Again, the referencing system favoured by your department would determine how your work is referenced, but the in-text citation could be:

(Stephen Murphy, 8 August 1972)

The main objective is to ensure that anyone following up on your research can find the same material you explored. Citing your research as fully as possible is good practice and working with un-catalogued material often requires a high level of detail.

Using archive material

As with any material, when you examine it, you should ask questions about its provenance and note down as much information as you can. You should record the author of any documents and their official title and role. You should try and identify who the key players are within the correspondence. If it is helpful to do so you could précis the correspondence or the report and copy down any relevant paragraphs or comments verbatim to be used in your own research.

If you cannot seem to find what you are looking for within the material, consider why this is. Are the files you are looking at the only place where such information could be stored? If you are looking at the director's personal papers then think about the other personnel who worked on the film who may have kept material from the production. What about the producer, members of the cast or the financier funding the production? If things are missing which should be present, then think about where the material could be. Can you track down the other half of important correspondence within industry organisations or in personal papers? The BBFC's defence of its classification of *A Clockwork Orange* (1971) was sent to a number of local councils in 1972, but no copy remains in the BBFC file. But a file in The National Archives does contain a copy of this lengthy and explosive letter as it was sent from one of Leeds' city councillors to the home secretary to protest about the BBFC's tone in the letter. Working with archival material means considering where the material may have ended up and tracking it down. This detective work can yield exciting results but may also require a great deal of hard work to locate anything of interest. You may have to make a number of trips to an archive before you find anything significant. You also cannot assume that archive material is going to offer revelatory findings which will directly benefit your research.

As a researcher, you should think about how you will use the material you find. You may discover exciting snippets of information, scandal or gossip. You may be reading passages from old letters between friends where certain things were written which could be embarrassing if made public. Being a researcher means conducting your research in an ethical manner; sometimes it is not the fact that you have found something that matters but how you will use it. If it is part of your research – for example, if it is a letter from Hitchcock discussing the appeal of a number of actresses he is considering casting in *Marnie* (1964) – then it could be relevant and worth reproducing. However, if the letter is a personal attack on a specific actress and her limited acting abilities, then you should consider what purpose it would serve to use such information. You can always allude to such information or reference non-contentious parts of the correspondence, but including material which is hurtful, explosive or damaging and which does not directly relate to your research can be unethical. If you have signed an agreement with the archive which owns the material then it may restrict you from publishing anything which would be damaging to the individual involved. As with all cases like this, it is a matter of judgement.

In addition to these ethical considerations, you should also be aware of issues of data protection. If you are keen to use material featured in letters from members of the public – for example, people who have written to their MP, respondents who have provided information as part of a social survey, or those who wrote letters of complaint to local councils – you should make sure that the people are not named. It is enough to note, 'this female respondent suggested ...' or 'a father of two wrote ...' or even 'a viewer from Bath complained that ...'. Such phrases do not weaken your work but ensure that the authors of the material you are using are protected. However, if the material is written by someone holding public office or a well-known figure, then naming them may be appropriate. For example, the prime minister, MPs, church leaders, the head of the Cinematograph Film Council, academics carrying out research, film directors, producers or industry figures, the head of the BBFC or the BFI can all be named. You should always consider whether naming the individual is important for your research. If your argument relies upon the fact that it is someone specific writing about a particular film or issue then it is appropriate to name them. Concerns about data protection are less of an issue for undergraduate work but can become problematic when working at MA or PhD level and when your work is being published.

FINANCIAL MATERIAL

As previous chapters have indicated, understanding the financial realities of different film industries and how and why different films are made relies upon financial data. Often this data will have been retained, perhaps by financiers, management companies, government or industry funding bodies or by the producer or director themselves. When accessing records like this you need to have a clear idea of what you want to find out and how the financial material can help you. You must also be aware of its limitations.

Some financial data can help to give you an insight, an overview or an indication of film popularity, production costs or profit and loss, but such information needs to be carefully contextualised. All film companies will have had financial records and accounts but they may not have been retained. Some film production companies were set up to fund specific films, or to support the work of particular directors or producers. They may have been short lived and the records may have subsequently disappeared. This is particularly true for the parts of the film industry which are very poorly documented, such as low-budget films or pornography.

When confronted with financial data you need first to consider what it is showing you. Can you draw conclusions about the success or failure of a film from the data provided? Where have the data come from and why have they been retained? Is it a record of payments from the Eady levy fund, which indicates a level of success at the British box office, or it is an account of how much money was spent on advertising or marketing the film? Are the financial figures included in an end-of-year report or account? Copies of the National Film Finance Corporation end-of-year accounts are held at the BFI Library and reveal an overview of the work of this organisation in selecting projects to fund and the level of success enjoyed. If you are looking at lists of popular films or the most successful films at the box office, consider where the information has come from and what it relates to. Does it relate only to cinemas in the London area, or to an individual cinema? Is it a global picture or a national one? Does it relate to British films in America or is it all films released in the US in the period covered by the records? If the records are historical then you need to take note of fluctuations and variations caused by inflation and price increases, while if they are contemporary and posted online you should try and verify them with a range of other sources. Are the accounts part of a corporation or organisation's financial records, or have they been retained by an individual?

You should be careful about making substantial claims based solely on financial records. The records may only be partially complete, and key sections may be missing. If you have found financial data in the company records or accounts, can this data be corroborated by a different source, for example from the director's own personal papers, or from the records of the NFFC or the BFI? Beware of using information found on Wikipedia or the Internet Movie Data Base (IMDB): the financial claims made on these websites can be difficult to verify. Interviews with the director or producer when a film has been completed will often contain basic financial information which will give you a rough idea of costs involved, but in cases like this it can be a good idea to indicate where the figures have come from when you present the information. For example, you could note, 'In an interview with *Total Film*, the director recalled that the film's budget was ...'. This indicates that it is simply the director's recollection of these figures rather than hard financial data.

Sometimes financial records include details of cast salaries – usually one of the biggest costs in filmmaking. These figures can be illuminating and can offer insights into how the industry operates at a particular time, as well as the individual value of specific stars. Sometimes these figures can be surprising. For example, the Carry On series of films was based around an ensemble cast with familiar faces, including Hattie Jacques, Barbara Windsor, Sid James and Kenneth Williams. Yet the production and salary information held in Peter Rogers' papers at the BFI reveals that not all of the cast were paid equally for their work on the films and that James and Williams were paid significantly more than the rest of the cast on the later films. The files also indicate that the company had to take out specific health insurance in order to employ Hattie Jacques for the later films due to her declining health. These snippets of financial information can be used to explore further the production context of the Carry On series. Rogers' papers also indicate how much was spent on each film; the majority of the films were funded by J. Arthur Rank productions, until *Carry On England* (1976) was deemed too expensive and so Rogers and Thomas applied to the NFFC and to EMI to fund the film. The escalating costs for each film and the increasingly complex funding arrangements for the final instalments in the series indicate how film funding was changing, and how and why the industry ultimately became reluctant to fund new films in a once-popular series.

Discovering some relevant financial information can be useful but be careful not to get too bogged down in the facts and figures. Unless you are a trained accountant or financial analyst, the figures may be difficult to understand and you should perhaps think about the ways in which the information can be useful for your research rather than spending time trying to understand the intricacies of film finance.

ORAL SOURCES: RECORDED INTERVIEWS

Recorded interviews with film industry figures can provide you with great research material, but you must consider a range of things before using it. Specifically, you need to think about when the material was recorded and whether the interview was designed to publicise a new project or recorded to celebrate someone's achievements. Where was it shown or broadcast? Is it part of a broader collection and, if so, how was this collection funded and is it attached to a particular project? What are the objectives of the project and how might this have influenced the interview itself? Has the material been digitised and can it be accessed as sound files? If it remains on VHS tapes or cassettes, where can it be accessed, and are there facilities to view it or listen to it? Finally, if the raw material is not available, are there interview transcripts which can be accessed?

Crucially, you must also take into account how much time has elapsed since the events being described and the interview itself. Interviews can yield fascinating information, yet they cannot be held to be a true account of past events, particularly if the events being discussed took place many years previously. Memory is fallible and people may retell events according to their own particular perspective. This does not make the material worthless – quite the contrary – but again, ideas of subjectivity, bias, opinion, memory and purpose must all be discussed in relation to recorded interviews. If you are interested in using recorded interviews as part of your research then you should pay due attention to methodologies concerned with oral and recorded histories.

As film is such a young discipline, it is always possible that the people you are researching are still alive and may be willing to talk with you about the filmmaking process and to offer you their own memories of events.

Conducting your own interviews

Conducting interviews with people in the film industry or those now retired from the industry can give you some fantastic material. Most people can be reached via agents or companies and some will have their own websites with ways to contact them. Or you can track down people through shared contacts. The format of the interview – email, in person, over the phone – will determine what kind of responses you get. For example, if you email someone a list of questions, it is easy for them to give you one-word responses or to avoid questions which they do not want to answer. On the telephone you have more opportunity to build a rapport with someone and can ask them to develop their responses or follow up interesting comments, but you will be unable to respond to any visual signs or body language. Conducting an interview in person is a great opportunity, but you need to think about what you ask and how you ask it. If you ask the wrong questions or alienate your respondent then you may not gather anything of particular use; they may refuse to answer any more questions or take the discussion in a different direction.

All interviews are different but there are a few key things that you should consider:

- **Be prepared**: Do your homework and make sure that you have a good understanding of the person you are interviewing, their body of work and their career. When interviewing, you need to demonstrate that you have a working knowledge of your topic. If you ask obvious or naive questions, your interviewee may become frustrated, bored or annoyed.
- **Avoid asking personal questions or looking for 'off the record' comments**: It is unlikely they will want to answer questions like this and even if they do, you need to think about how it is relevant to your research.
- **Do ask if you can record the interview**: If they give their consent then agree with them that you will type up the transcript of the interview or check their responses with them before using it in your research. Giving them final approval on what they have said is good research practice.
- When you compose your interview questions, think about what you want to find out and how to elicit this information. Be aware that asking open questions can break the ice, but they can also

elicit a great deal of unfocused or generic information. You should be prepared to use a combination of general and specific, open and closed questions to gain information.

- **It is usually best to begin with a discursive question and to explain your research interest:** For example, you may want to explore the film industry in the 1990s and are asking director Danny Boyle how difficult it was to get funding for *Shallow Grave* and what motivated him to work with Film Four.
- **Be wary of your interviewee taking control of the interview:** Some people are used to being interviewed and may only wish to talk about specific aspects of their work.
- **Be gracious and polite:** Let your enthusiasm for your research and the topic come through the interview but do not gush or be star struck.
- **Be aware that your interviewee may not want to answer a question:** If this happens or if they are uncomfortable with a line of questioning, then you need to respect that and move on.
- **Be careful not to lead the interview in a particular direction:** Avoid leading questions and try and let your interviewee offer their own explanations and responses in their own words. It is much better for them to offer their opinions and views rather than to simply confirm what you have said.
- **Be aware that your interviewee's memory of events may not match other accounts:** If you are enquiring about events which took place a while ago, your respondent's memories of the event may be different from what is popularly believed to have happened. Events are always remembered from different perspectives and may be shaped by subsequent events. For example, if you are interviewing a director about a producer he worked with ten years ago and with whom they have since fallen out, the memories of the project they worked on together will be informed by their subsequent feelings about each other.
- **Be sensitive to past events:** Asking for details about why someone filed for bankruptcy or querying if the press criticism of a specific film was particularly painful may be uncomfortable topics which your respondent may not want to discuss. If you have established a rapport with your interviewee then you may be able to frame such questions in a sensitive and inoffensive manner. For example, 'I imagine that criticism of the film was quite a shock. Were you surprised by the reactions to the film?' or 'What do you remember

about the press response to the film's release, and could you tell
me a little bit about your own reactions?'

Online data gathering

If you are keen to gather some audience data or to set up a web survey
to help you elicit responses to a particular film then you could either
find a way of collecting information from people in person or set up an
online questionnaire. Setting up a questionnaire, survey or discussion
space online may generate more data than standing outside the cinema
with a clipboard but there are a range of things that you need to
consider.

An online questionnaire or survey needs to be presented in the
best possible way and to target the most useful respondents. If you are
surveying teen attitudes towards cinema certification, for example the
difference between the 15 and the 18 certificates, think about what
kinds of questions you need to ask. You will need basic demographic
information such as age and gender, but you should also include
questions which allow respondents to respond quickly with their own
opinions or perhaps include a series of options to enable them to
provide their answers. Using a mixture of statement questions and
open responses could provide you with some interesting data. Before
including any questions on your survey you should think about the kind
of data you want to gather. If you want to ask questions about audience
experience then you need to offer a range of options so people can
indicate their preferred response, but you may also want to include a
comment space so people can add their own thoughts. You should avoid
using completely closed questions and you should make sure that your
questions are well phrased and easy to understand. Avoid repetition and
double negatives and have someone else look over your questions to
make sure that they make sense before you activate the survey.

If you are keen to begin this kind of work you should take note of
how other researchers have undertaken their own data collection. Justin
Smith's work on web forums and cult films and Emma Pett's analysis of
audience responses to a special screening of *Back to the Future* (1985)
offer different models of how to carry out this kind of work and can
help you think carefully about your own methodology and approach.[3]

If you decide to set up your survey online you should also think about
how to get people to answer the survey and where it will be hosted.

Survey site surveymonkey allows you to set up a free questionnaire of ten questions, and potential respondents can be sent a link to the survey.[4] You should consider whether you can include the link in an email sent round to friends and ask them to pass it on. Can you use any existing mailing lists to reach a broader range of potential respondents? Are there social networks or online forums you can use to help you circulate your survey? If you are keen to survey a broader range of people rather than just your peer group, you will need to think of strategies to help you do this. Perhaps you can work with your local cinema and hand out postcards with the web address of the survey to cinema audiences? How you decide to carry out this research will again depend on the research question and what you want to explore.

ONLINE SOURCES

As already noted above in relation to web sources, you need to think carefully about using moving image material found online and have a clear understanding of how the material was made and who it is made for. You should also consider how you will use the material to explore your research question. The same considerations apply with online written sources as with online visual sources, and much of what has already been noted about conventional offline sources also applies to online material. For example, online critiques and reviews of films can be very useful, but it can be difficult to differentiate critical, useful reviews from opinion pieces and personal blogs which have less value as objective sources. You may know very little about the person posting or writing the review and they may be writing from a personal rather than a professional or critical viewpoint. However, this does not mean that their critique is worthless, but rather – as with all sources – you should acknowledge its inconsistencies and its bias and then explore it in relation to a range of other sources. For instance, you could compare published reviews of a specific film with comments and responses posted online to explore the difference between fan attitudes and industry attitudes. Such an approach would allow you to explore the responses to the film but also to acknowledge the different ways in which film can be written about and how all this material can be used to explore audience response.

Using web forums to investigate online attitudes to various film-related issues, such as casting a popular franchise or the ending of a trilogy, again offers great possibilities. If you choose to utilise these kinds of sources, you must remain objective and consider how your methodology will allow you to explore the material, ask pertinent questions of the comments and of those making the comments and consider how all of this work will contribute to your overall research question. It is not enough simply to search for responses to the latest Batman film and use the comments as quotes. You need to employ skills of discourse analysis, just as you would when examining newspaper or magazine material.

CONCLUSION

When you undertake your research you should always bear your research question firmly in mind. You need to be aware of what you are trying to find out so that you do not become so entangled in your sources – either written or visual – that you can no longer be objective and lose sight of your aims. The further reading indicated below can help you to approach your sources more specifically and the methodology and approach you will need to adopt to carry out your research effectively.

NOTES

1 Jean Burgess and Joshua Green, *YouTube*, Digital Media and Society series (Cambridge: Polity Press, 2009).
2 Ciara Chambers, *Ireland in the Newsreels* (Dublin: Irish Academic Press, 2012); Luke McKernan (ed.), *Yesterday's News: The British Cinema Newsreel Reader* (London: BUFVC Press, 2002).
3 Smith, *Withnail and Us*; Emma Pett "'Hey! Hey! I've seen this one, I've seen this one. It's a classic!'": nostalgia, repeat viewing and cult performance in *Back to the Future*', *Participations: Journal of Audience and Perception Studies* 10:1 (May 2013), www.participations.org/Volume%2010/Issue%201/11%20Pett%2010.1.pdf (accessed 14 October 2014).
4 www.surveymonkey.com.

RECOMMENDED FURTHER READING

Barber, Sarah and Peniston-Bird, Corinna (eds.), *History Beyond the Text: A Student's Guide to Approaching Alternative Sources* (London: Routledge, 2009).

Bloch, Marc, *The Historian's Craft*, trans. Peter Putnam, preface by Peter Burke (Manchester: Manchester University Press, 1992).

Gillham, Bill, *The Research Interview* (London: Continuum, 2000).

Green, Anna and Troup, Kathleen, *The Houses of History: A Critical Reader in Twentieth-Century History and Theory* (Manchester: Manchester University Press, 1999).

Jordanova, Ludmilla, *History in Practice*, 2nd edition (London: Hodder Arnold, 2006).

Machin David and Mayr, Andrea, *How to Do Critical Discourse Analysis: A Multimodal Introduction* (London: Sage, 2012).

Tosh, John, *The Pursuit of History: Aims, Methods and New Directions in the Study of Modern History*, 4th edition, (Harlow: Pearson Longman, 2006).

WEBSITES

www.surveymonkey.com.

9

WRITING UP YOUR FINDINGS

When it comes to writing up your research, there is no set formula to help you get it right, but there are things that you can do to ensure that your work is well presented, well structured and your arguments coherent and engaging. Unlike in the sciences, where the writing-up of formal experiments and lab work happens after all research is complete, research and writing in the arts and humanities can often be more fluid. For example, it may be the case that you are writing your essay and then discover some important material which needs to be included in your final work. Or it may be that you conclude all your research, write a first draft and then go through a series of revisions, developing your ideas and arguments as you go. Perhaps you begin by researching one area and then find that your research is taking you in a different direction and so will have to adjust your analysis and conclusions – and even your introduction and methodology – accordingly. If you are writing a longer piece of work like an MA or PhD thesis then you may be researching and writing up individual chapters before pulling it all together in the final months of your period of study.

Of course, writing up any kind of work requires time management and planning, but you also need to know what to include in your analysis and how to present it. This chapter will offer advice on how to write up your research in an academic way, how to structure your work, how you should undertake and present your analysis, how to explain your methodology and your review of literature and how to reference. Each of the following sections will include detailed examples of how you can present your work in the best way possible.

BEFORE YOU BEGIN

Before you begin the process of writing you should make a plan and detail how you will present your research findings. Having a clear idea of what you will cover, how your findings will be arranged, how your sources will be explored and how your methodology will be explained will ensure your work is coherent. The plan does not have to be very long and can of course be altered as your research develops, but planning your work is good practice, and an effective plan can be useful for all types of written work, from exam essays to dissertations.

You should always make sure that your plan is realistic and makes allowance for any time limitations. There is no point planning to visit archives or to make detailed primary research the basis of your analysis if you do not have the time to do it. Previous chapters have suggested how you can access and use a range of sources, and planning your work can be a real asset in helping you to see what is possible and what is too ambitious, what should be removed from your planned work and what needs to be expanded.

Much of this advice may seem very obvious, but it is easy to get carried away when writing an essay or a dissertation. One of the main problems may be that you are attempting to cover too much or being too ambitious in your scope. Other problems can be failing to be objective or devoting too much space in your work to the wrong thing, such as retelling the narrative of individual films, including too much background detail or far too much basic description.

WRITING STYLE AND TONE

Your university department will have a style guide for written pieces of work and you should consult this before submitting any work. Each module, unit or class may also have its own style guide. This is usually written by the person delivering the course and this is the person who is likely to be marking your written work. Avoid losing marks for style by making sure that you read these specific criteria and ensure that what you submit meets the standard guidelines. As well as the guidelines issued by your university or department, here are some general things to bear in mind when you are writing up your findings.

The first thing to remember is always to write in a formal style. You are writing for an academic audience and you should write accordingly. You should avoid using colloquialisms and informal language. One of the key things to remember is that although you may be writing about superhero movies, popular culture, historical epics, fandom or audiences, you need to ensure that the tone of your work is critical and analytical. Avoid writing like a journalist, an online blogger or a film critic. You must make sure you write in formal, grammatical sentences. Avoid abbreviating when you write; often abbreviations are too informal and make your work too conversational. Try and write in full; for example, use 'does not' instead of 'doesn't' or 'could have' rather than 'could've.'

Avoid writing in an overly complicated way. Never worry that the way you write is too simplistic; it is far better to be understood than to write in convoluted sentences which may not make sense. If you cannot see where you are going wrong with your grammar or phrasing then try reading your work aloud; if you find yourself stumbling over phrases or needing to draw breath in the middle of a sentence, then something is probably not right and needs to be changed. Reading articles, books and chapters of academic work will provide you with a useful style model. You should use these kinds of writings as the model for your academic writing rather than websites, blogs or magazine articles.

Avoid using 'I think' in your written work. You must remain objective; simply voicing your own opinions will not help in the presentation of your ideas and research. It is far better to use phrases such as 'the evidence suggests', 'my research has indicated', 'these findings demonstrate', 'it is possible to conclude' or 'this exploration reveals'. These observations will allow you to offer critical and thoughtful conclusions on your research findings but will ensure that you remain objective. Using 'I think' or 'I believe' in an essay really should be avoided.

Make sure that you do not make claims you cannot support. Avoid **sweeping statements** and observations which are unsubstantiated. You should also be realistic about what you can achieve. For example, it is unlikely that you will be able to prove conclusively that films made in the 1920s made people think or behave in a particular way. It is also not realistic to claim that blockbusters changed the world or that television was not very entertaining before HBO. Such statements are far too straightforward and should always be nuanced. For example, instead of 'Everyone in 1950s America was moving to the suburbs and buying a television,' try 'One of the dominant trends in 1950s America was a move to the suburbs driven by a number of social and economic changes.' This claim should then be supported by a piece of evidence which can be referenced, for example 'Dawson notes that in this period, television ownership grew more than 130 per cent.' It is far better to present your findings as examinations, analysis or explorations which can be supported by evidence rather than simply a statement of what you know or what you think you know.

STRUCTURING YOUR WORK

Often it is not the level of effort or the research undertaken which lets down a piece of work, but rather the way in which it is structured and arranged. If your ideas appear haphazard and your analysis scattered without logical development, then your work will not be well received. As mentioned above, it is useful to plan your work and have a clear idea of what you will include within your essay, report or dissertation. Here are some basic tips on structuring your work.

Firstly, you need to establish **what kind of work** it is and what structure would be most appropriate. Are there formal requirements about structure which are part of the assessment criteria? If it is an essay then the structure will be simpler than if it is a report or a critical review. In an essay you may be able to write using sub-headings or chapters, while the format of a report could require you to outline your methodology for carrying out interviews or working through archive material as a separate methodology section. If it is appropriate to do so you can always include images, charts, graphs or tables to help detail your findings, but again this will depend on the kind of work you are undertaking. Alternatively, it might be essential that you write in straightforward prose without sub-headings, bullet points or chapters to help organise your results and findings. If this is the case then it is essential that your arguments evolve throughout your work in a logical and fluent manner.

Secondly, whatever the piece of work, you will need an **introduction.** This should outline your intentions within the work and indicate how you will be approaching the topic. You should use the introduction to address any contested ideas within the question. For example, the question 'Using two examples, explore the representation of women within films of the British new wave' requires you to explore the issues of gender and representation within a set body of films known as the 'British new wave'. In your introduction you should briefly address the concept of the 'British new wave' and try and define this term. It may be that definitions vary, some perhaps suggesting that British new wave films make up a genre or cycle, others arguing that it is a label applied to a disparate collection of films which were made in the same period and which share some visual and textual characteristics but which cannot be easily identified as a cohesive body of films. It is important that the problems of definition are identified within your introduction to indicate how you will be approaching the subject and that you are aware of the complexities of the question.

Following on from your introduction, you should now indicate precisely how you went about this work. In a report which draws upon quantitative or qualitative research carried out, such as interviews or questionnaires, you need to **define your methodology** in detail. For example, how many respondents did you have, how did you contact them, was their selection random or were you seeking respondents who fell into a particular age bracket? If your work is an essay your methodology will be more critical, theoretical or conceptual. On the above question relating to women in the British new wave, you will need to use your methodology to detail which films you will be focusing on and why. Have you chosen one film with a female protagonist and one with a strong supporting female cast in order to compare and contrast representations? Or have you selected one film from the earliest years of the new wave and one from the final years so that you can contrast their representations and map change over time? Are you comparing films made by the same director, or films set in the same location?

You should also define which specific **critical approach** you will be using within your work. Are you exploring representations of women within the British new wave from a feminist perspective using the critique provided by Molly Haskell or Laura Mulvey? Or is this too specific to Hollywood and does not fit easily within explorations of British cinema? Are you choosing to ground your analysis on work done on British cinema and gender, such as Moya Luckett's exploration of swinging London and extending this analysis to include the British new wave? Maybe you are keen to use Freudian theory combined with close textual analysis to help you explore the question of gendered representation? Perhaps you are drawing on the work undertaken on the British new wave and masculinity to see how this approach could be adapted to suit an exploration of feminine identity?

Whatever approach you decide upon, you need to justify it to your reader within your methodology towards the start of your work; it is no good leaving the methodological and critical justifications until mid-way through the essay. They should be clarified at the earliest opportunity.

A key part of any work will be **a review of existing literature**. For any essay which asks you to explore key themes, concepts or ideas, you will need to consider what has already been written and to consider how it can be used within your own work. For example, a case study of *Bonnie and Clyde* will need to draw attention to the fact that the film emerges as part of the tradition of 'new Hollywood' in the late 1960s. Books and articles which pertain to the film and to the concept of new Hollywood should be referred to and used to help answer the question. A review of literature or a literature survey should demonstrate to your reader that you are aware of the important works published in the relevant field and that you understand the work already undertaken. An exploration of 1960s British cinema should refer to work by Robert Murphy and Alexander Walker, while work on the British horror film needs to reference publications by Steve Chibnall, Julian Petley and Peter Hutchings. You do not need to write a review of each book, chapter or article but you do need to show how such work has influenced the field and how you will use it in your own work. For example, in an essay on the British horror film you could observe:

> A great deal has been written on Hammer horror, notably by Peter Hutchings, yet the revival of Hammer horror as a brand in recent years has only recently begun to be addressed.

Or,

> It has been the trend within writing on British horror cinema to identify the key players within the field, such as Steve Chibnall's work on Peter Walker or Peter Hutchings' study of Terence Fisher, but what of more modern directors who work within the horror film genre? How does a film like *28 Days Later* (2002) fit within the established conventions and traditions of British horror cinema?

As well as offering a review of all the relevant literature, writing in this way will also help you to identify the sources you have used in your work. What are the key sources? Are they the films themselves, archival footage, financial ledgers or documents which pertain to part of the industry, audience responses or fan letters in a magazine? You will probably consult a selection of sources, written and visual, primary and secondary. Again you do not be need to go into extreme detail about each individual source, but it is useful to indicate the range of sources you have consulted and also to point out and identify any omissions. For example, you may have undertaken close textual, visual and content analysis on Pathé newsreel films of the 1940s yet have been unable to find any newsreels from 1942 as they are unaccountably missing from the Pathé online database. Rather than simply ignoring this omission and hoping that your reader will not notice, it is far better to speculate briefly on this absence and indicate how it has shaped your research. Of course, the absence or availability of material may also have informed your methodology and will in itself shape your analysis and conclusions.

Once you have undertaken your analysis, answered the question and presented your research in a series of thoughtful arguments, you will need to draw your work together in a **conclusion.** All work needs a conclusion, whether it is an essay, a report, a dissertation or a critique. There are a couple of things you should remember when you write your conclusion.

Firstly, it should not be excessively long. Remember, your conclusion is the closing part of the work; it should not be very detailed and should not recap everything that you have already written about. Try and avoid repetition of previous arguments and keep it brief and to the point.

Do not introduce new material into your conclusion. If material is important enough to be included within your work, then it should be incorporated into your analysis. You should also avoid using quotations in your conclusion. More than any other part of your work, your conclusion should be based upon your own work and findings. You should still avoid 'I think' and instead refer to the analysis you have undertaken: for example ,'As my research has shown ...' or 'My analysis has identified ...'. Such phrases indicate that you are basing your concluding remarks on work you have carried out, not on vague ideas, general observations or other people's research.

Your conclusion should highlight the important aspects of your research and your key findings, drawing attention to how these relate back to the original question. A good conclusion will refer back to the terms of the question and indicate how your work has addressed it. For example, a useful conclusion could begin:

> This discussion of national identity in the films of David Lean has revealed a number of key ideas. As my research has shown, it is possible to see how Lean's explorations of 'Britishness' shifted from the working-class solidarity and straightforward patriotic decency of the Gibbons family in *This Happy Breed* to the thorny discussions of Irish and English nationalism in *Ryan's Daughter*. However, as my analysis has revealed, it is also crucial to map these developing representations of filmic national identity alongside broader social, political and economic changes taking place within the period 1940–1970.

Within your conclusion you should be very careful not to over-state what you have discovered. It is highly unlikely that you have 'proved' anything beyond a shadow of a doubt and you should instead view your work as offering a discussion or analysis of an interesting question or idea rather than offering a solution. If appropriate, it may also be a good idea to indicate what else remains to be done in a particular area of research. If you have explored gendered discourses on British television in the 1960s, you could suggest to what extent your work would be useful to help consider such discourses in later decades, or within a different medium like film, or within a different context, such as American television in the same period. It is useful to indicate to your reader the limits of what you have explored and how your work could be developed and expanded.

Structuring your work in the way indicated above should help you make sure your findings are focused and to the point. Of course, the most important aspect of your work is the research you have carried out and how you shape this into detailed and thoughtful analysis.

ANALYSIS

Your analysis should always explore and answer the question posed, using the sources, methodology and critical framework you have identified. As a visual subject, analysis of films, television, YouTube clips, amateur films or newsreels is likely to be central to your research. An earlier chapter has indicated how to analyse a film or visual text, while this section is concerned with how best to articulate that analysis. As close textual and visual analysis may be subjective you should always ensure that you personal observations and analysis can be supported.

One of the first things you need to do is think carefully about the terms of the question: are you being asked to compare, analyse, explore, discuss, consider or evaluate? What precisely are you being asked to study? You need to understand what is specifically indicated within the question and what is implied. If the question asks you to discuss the impact of technology on the visual style of films of new Hollywood then you have to address technological innovation, visual style and new Hollywood *and also* explore how all these separate elements relate to one another. For example, if changes in technology led to more innovative camerawork and cinematography, then you need to identify how this affected visual style in particular films. You cannot simply write, 'camerawork became more innovative in the films of New Hollywood'. You need to write something like:

The developments and improvements in lighting and camerawork had a substantial impact on films made during the period of 'new Hollywood'. These changes can be discerned in the unique visual style of films such as *Chinatown* and *Raging Bull*. The boxing sequences in the latter film were shot using steadicam technology, and the increased mobility of the camera allows for the fight scenes to be filmed by the camera operator as if the camera was in the ring with the boxers. Geoff King considers that changes in technology were a crucial part of the development of new Hollywood ...

You should also make sure that all concepts you use are adequately defined. 'New Hollywood', 'British new wave', 'cinema verité', 'feminist filmmaking' are all concepts which need to be defined. As shown in the earlier chapter on theory and methodology, different scholars, critics and theorists will have different definitions and understanding of these terms and it is important to identify these variances in terminology. It is also worth considering that filmmakers may not have the same understanding of a scholarly concept as a researcher. It would be unwise to claim that the 1960s documentary filmmakers the Maysles brothers were keen to explore ideas of 'cinema verité' or 'cinema of truth' within their work if you do not have any firm evidence to support this assertion. This is also an issue of historiography; much of the formal film studies terminology came into existence much later than the films to which they have been applied. Applying these terms retrospectively can be useful but you need to be aware of the problems in doing so. Within your analysis, you must make sure that you select your terms carefully. As well as defining your terms you should be careful not to make casual use of value-laden or 'loaded' terms which can carry completely different meanings. For example, if you are writing about film and audiences and you use terms such as 'signification' or 'transference' or 'cognition', you need to be aware that these terms mean different things in different fields. If you do not mean to use them in a psychological or psychoanalytic context then you need to make this clear and you should always define your terms at the start of your research. This can be done succinctly, and a covering statement which notes, 'All the terms within this work relate to notions of psychoanalysis and draw upon the critiques of Freud and Lacan, paying particular attention to their work on signification, can be applied to a range of 1940 films' should be sufficient.

As already identified, the structure of your work is very important. Your ideas should follow on logically from one another and should be linked together. As suggested above, you should make a plan and stick to it. This should help you see what needs to be included and how it all fits together. For example, if the question requires you to explore character, narrative and visual style in two different films then you must make sure that you offer full analysis of all three elements and be certain that this analysis applies to both films. You could do this in a number of ways. You could explore and analyse all these elements within one film in the first part of the essay, then explore all the same elements within the second film in the second part of the essay. The final part of the essay could draw this analysis together with an exploration of points of similarity and difference between the two films. Or you could explore character in both films in the first section, discuss narrative in both films in the second section and then finally examine the visual style of both films in the third section of the essay, followed by a conclusion. This structure would allow you to compare and contrast the two selected films through the essay and could allow for a deeper exploration of the terms of the question. However, the decision you make regarding the structure of your work may depend on the material you are dealing with, how many words you have in order to address the subject and the sophistication and detail of your analysis.

You should also remember that context is important. Avoid discussing films as abstract concepts that exist in a vacuum. Cinema-going is a cultural activity and film is a crafted product and the exploration of any film or cycle of films should refer to the period in which they were made. Some questions may require more in the way of contextual detail and exploration. For example, if the question is about the Warner Bros gangster film cycle of the 1930s and anxieties about screen violence in Depression-era America, then you need to find a way to relate the textual (the films) to the broader historical content (the Great Depression) and cultural and social anxieties (about violence). To do this you could perhaps sketch in the historical context of Depression era America, the popularity of the cinema in this period, specifically drawing attention to gangster films, and how and why concerns about screen violence and behaviour were becoming more vocal. After drawing on contemporary reports and newspaper articles about violence and the cinema you could offer a series of case studies looking at a selection of gangster films from the 1930s and how they present violence. Textual analysis of these films could be supported by a study of contemporary reviews, letters to newspapers and government legislation and, of course, supplemented by critical work undertaken on these films and the period by other scholars.

You must make sure that what you offer is analysis rather than description. Avoid retelling the narratives of films or explaining the events of a particular decade or period in a straightforward and uncritical way. When offering analysis, you need to make sure your observations are fully supported. Try and relate your analysis back to the question. If you are exploring representations of class within a range of 1980s British films, then you need to offer specific analysis of key moments in these films. The more specific you can be, the better your analysis will be. Instead of simply pointing out that a particular scene deals with issues of class, you need to identify precisely how it does this. Is it through camerawork, lighting, setting, mise-en-scene, costumes, dialogue, narrative or character performance? Why is class so important at this particular moment in the film? Does it move the narrative forward, and if so why is this important? Good analysis will link your ideas to specific and precise examples, supported by secondary material rather than relying on dialogue or descriptions of the film scenes.

When it comes to visual analysis, a great deal may be based on your own thoughts and interpretations, but you must support your claims with evidence. It is not enough simply to say, 'The use of lighting and camera angles in *Mildred Pierce* contribute to an overall effect of film noir'. Instead you could write:

> The chiaroscuro lighting within *Mildred Pierce*, such as that evident in the opening scenes at the beach and then later in the police station, focuses on the title character, bathing her with sharp light which picks out her angular features pulled taught with tension, while the rest of the set is in darkness. As Alain Silver remind us, such effects are typical of Hollywood film noir, and in the case of this particular film work indicate both the narrative tension within this particular scene and the moral ambiguity of Mildred's motivation.

The above example should also include a reference to Silver's work in a footnote or an in-text citation.

You should ensure that everything you include is relevant to the question. If you have a good plan and structure your work well then this should prevent you from including extraneous and irrelevant material. Writing an essay on the films of David Lynch may require some exploration of Lynch as a filmmaker but a full biography of David Lynch as an individual will probably not be relevant. Similarly, if you are using American films of the 1950s to explore changing attitudes to promiscuity, sexuality and youth, you do not need to include a vast amount of material on the history of promiscuous behaviour and teen sexuality in America, but rather include contextual material where appropriate, clearly focused on the period in question.

You should also think about what you have discovered throughout the research process. It is unlikely that you have simply confirmed everything that you already knew, so make the most of what you have discovered, flagging up key findings and how these can help our understanding of a particular issue. Make it clear what you have discovered and what your research demonstrates. As with all academic work, all assertions and analysis must be supported by a range of evidence and you can qualify what you have discovered to make it clear how your work contributes to an existing debate but that more remains to be done.

Do not worry if your work does not seem to be original. It is very unlikely that your research will explore a topic which no one else has ever studied, particularly if it is research related to a topic you are studying as part of a course or module. But your work can help to contribute to an existing debate, set of questions or ideas, as well as demonstrating how a specific theory can be used or revealing how detailed technical knowledge can allow for thoughtful and insightful observations. If you adopted an approach which challenged existing conceptions of understandings of a period, then this will help with the critical reappraisal of that period. If you used a new theoretical model to address a familiar body of films then you may have new insights to offer but you may also have discovered why such an approach is less than useful. Such discoveries are simply part of the research process and can be briefly alluded to within your conclusion.

You should always be mindful and considerate of other people's work; just because someone else's work is different from your own does not mean that it is valueless. Similarly, just because you disagree with someone else's findings, research methodology or critical approach, it does not make it incorrect or flawed. It is far better to pay due attention to what existing work can offer to your own research, for example, you could observe:

> Leon Hunt's work pays particular attention to the low-budget end of British cinema, yet does not draw any firm conclusions about popular taste and audience. Exploring why these films were so popular is a key part of my own research, and Hunt's exploration of this topic offers a good introduction to low-budget cinema which my work will develop.

Avoid making simplistic judgements about the value and worth of other people's work. Such assertions are generally unhelpful and demonstrate your own lack of objectivity.

QUOTING AND REFERENCING

In any academic work, you must make sure that you quote from a range of critical sources. If your work has drawn upon primary material, such as letters, magazine articles, financial documents or newspaper entries, then you need to briefly explore how, when, where and why this material was written and what value it has. You do not need to perform detailed historical analysis on every source you include but you must demonstrate an understanding of why the range of material is important. For example, if you are using fan material from 1953, you need to think about where it was published, who wrote it and who may have read it. If it was published in a fan magazine devoted to the attractions of American teen film stars and mainly written and consumed by teenage girls then this material obviously relates to a very specific audience. While valuable in helping us to understand the teenage audience, it cannot be used to offer conclusions about 1950s audiences as a whole. Similarly, if you are using critical reviews of a film from British newspapers like *The Times* or the *Guardian*, you need to be aware of the particular target audience of these newspapers. Reviews in these newspapers will be very different to reviews of the same film published in the *Daily Mail* or the *Daily Mirror*. Again, you do not need to go into these differences in detail but you must show that you are aware of these variations in tone, address, intended audience, possible bias and nuance. Similarly, if you are looking at reviews of a single film across a period of time, then you should be aware of how external events can be shaping responses to a film. For example, wartime audiences may have revelled in the flourishing, rousing and patriotic *Henry V* (1944) and reviews may reflect this, while critics and audiences fifty years later may find the same film visually garish and narratively ponderous. Modern audiences will have different expectations from earlier cinemagoers and these altered audience expectations must be acknowledged in any discussion of material from different historical moments.

As well as research carried out in the archive, or from personal papers, ledgers or letters, secondary sources should be used to supplement your findings. Contextual detail should be provided using a range of sources. It is unlikely that you will just *know* about the development of silent film in the early years of the twentieth century: such information will have been culled from somewhere and should always be referenced accordingly. If you have gathered the basics from a lecture or a website then you should develop your knowledge by reading some scholarly work on the topic. Neither lecture notes, class handouts written by your teacher or Wikipedia entries are good sources to be cited in academic work. You should also avoid relying too much on a single sources. Film textbooks such as those by David Bordwell and Kristin Thompson (*Film Art: An Introduction*) and Timothy Corrigan and Patricia White (*The Film Experience*) can offer useful overviews of key periods, film styles, theories and movements and technical developments, but consulting these general texts should be the first stage of your research and more specific sources should be used to provide more detail.

Make sure that when you include quotations from either primary or secondary sources that these quotations help you to develop your arguments. Do not simply insert quotations in lieu of your own words; you must ensure that quotations develop, support, critique or contradict the point that you are making. Quotations also need to be properly introduced; for example, 'Ellis notes that ...' or 'Spicer draws attention to the importance of mise-en-scene when he argues ...'. You cannot simply insert quotations and let them 'speak' for themselves: they must be properly introduced. If you are using historical material, it is often useful to make this clear: for example, 'This letter from 1953 highlights the importance of film stars to the teen audience. Published in *Picturegoer* magazine, the author writes ...'

Referencing

There are a great many different referencing systems, and the kind you should use will depend on which system is favoured by your university or department. Depending on their preference, references in your written work will either be in-text citations or footnotes or endnotes. You must make sure that you follow the standards set by your department. Failing to acknowledge the work of others is plagiarism and can result in heavy penalties. Even if you are not quoting directly but rather referencing work as a whole or précising an argument, point of view or approach, you should always include a proper reference. For example, 'Martin Barker's work on the video-nasty provides a useful introduction to this topic.' This sentence should include a note or in-text reference to Barker's work to make it clear which of Barker's publications you are referring to.

You should be careful not to over-quote. Including lengthy quotations from someone else's work can suggest that you do not have any ideas of your own. Generally, quotations should be a few lines long and usually no more than a sentence. Of course, this will depend on the kind of work that you are doing, but you need to integrate the quotations into your work and use them to strengthen your arguments.

As well as citing and referencing the work within your essay, dissertation or report, you should include a list of references as a bibliography and a list of visual sources, online sources and filmography. This should be a comprehensive list of all the sources you consulted when researching. More information on how to cite and reference a variety of material can be obtained from a number of excellent citation guides, notably *Cite them Right*, published by Richard Pears and Graham Shields and the BUFVC's guide to citing audio-visual resources, which can be downloaded from their website.[1] Programmes to help you manage your footnotes and referencing such as Zotero and Endnote can be very useful but are really only appropriate for longer pieces of work.

CONCLUSION

This chapter has offered advice on how to present your research. However, each piece of work is different and you should remember that the approach outlined here is simply a model of good practice; more information on how to present your research will be offered as part of your course of study. Sessions on essay writing, using library resources and time management can really help you to develop your work and your ideas and will give you a clear indication of what is required of you by your institution and department. The final section of this work includes a bibliography which indicates what kind of detail you need to include with any piece of academic written work and how it should be set out.

NOTES

1   Richard Pears and Graham Shields, *Cite them Right: The Essential Referencing Guide*, 9th edition (Basingstoke: Palgrave Macmillan, 2013); 'Audiovisual citation: BUFVC guidelines for referencing moving image and sound', British Universities Film & Video Council. May 2013, http://bufvc.ac.uk/projects-research/avcitation (accessed 14 October 2014)

RECOMMENDED FURTHER READING

Corrigan, Timothy J., *A Short Guide to Writing About Film* (New York and London: Pearson Longman, 2007).

Gocsik, Karen and Barsam, Richard, *Writing About Movies* (New York: Norton, 2007).

Pears, Richard and Shields, Graham, *Cite them Right: The Essential Referencing Guide*, 9th edition (Basingstoke: Palgrave Macmillan, 2013).

Rudestam, Kjell, and Newton, Rae, *Surviving your Dissertation: A Comprehensive Guide to Content and Process*, 3rd edition (London: Sage, 2007).

Walliman, Nicholas, *Your Undergraduate Dissertation: The Essential Guide for Success* (London: Sage, 2004).

SELECT BIBLIOGRAPHY AND RESOURCES

BOOKS

Aaron, Michelle, *Spectatorship: The Power of Looking On* (London: Wallflower Press, 2007).

Aldgate, Anthony and Richards, Jeffrey, *Britain Can Take It: The British Cinema in the Second World War* (Edinburgh: Edinburgh University Press, 1994).

Aldgate, Anthony and Robertson, James C., *Censorship in Theatre and Cinema* (Edinburgh, Edinburgh University Press, 2005).

Allen, Robert C. and Gomery, Douglas, *Film History: Theory and Practice* (Boston, MA: McGraw-Hill, 1993).

Ashby, Justine and Higson, Andrew (eds.), *British Cinema, Past and Present* (London: Routledge, 2000).

Barber, Sarah and Penniston-Bird, Corinna M. (eds.), *History Beyond the Text: A Student's Guide to Approaching Alternative Sources* (Abingdon: Routledge, 2009).

Barber, Sian, *Censoring the 1970s: The BBFC and the Decade that Taste Forgot* (Newcastle: Cambridge Scholars Publishing, 2011).

Barber, Sian, *The British Film Industry in the 1970s: Capital, Culture and Creativity* (Basingstoke: Palgrave Macmillan, 2013).

Barker, Martin (ed.), *The Video Nasties: Freedom and Censorship in the Media* (London: Pluto Press, 1984).

Barr, Charles, *Ealing Studios* (Moffat: Cameron & Hollis, 1998).

Barta, Tony (ed.), *Screening the Past: Film and the Representation of History* (Westport, CT: Praeger, 1998).

Bazin, André, *What is Cinema?*, essays selected and trans. Hugh Gray, 2 vols (Berkeley, CA, and London: University of California Press, 2005).

Bell, Melanie, *Femininity in the Frame: Women and 1950s British Popular Cinema* (London: I.B. Tauris, 2009).

Bloch, Marc, *The Historian's Craft*, trans. Peter Putnam, preface by Peter Burke (Manchester: Manchester University Press, 1992).

Bordwell, David, *On the History of Film Style* (Cambridge, MA, and London: Harvard University Press, 1997).

Bordwell, David and Thompson, Kristin, *Film Art: An Introduction* (Boston, MA, and London: McGraw-Hill, 2004).

Bordwell, David and Thompson, Kristin, *Film History: An Introduction*, 3rd edition (New York: McGraw-Hill Higher Education, 2010).

Braudy, Leo, Cohen, Marshall and Mast, Gerald (eds.), *Film Theory and Criticism: Introductory Readings*, 4th edition (New York and Oxford: Oxford University Press, 1992).

Burgess, Jean and Green, Joshua, *YouTube*, Digital Media and Society series (Cambrdige: Polity Press, 2009).

Burke, Peter, *Varieties of Cultural History* (Cambridge: Polity Press, 1997).

Burrows, Elaine *et al.* (eds.), *The British Cinema Source Book: BFI Archive Viewing Copies and Library Materials* (London: BFI Publishing, 1995).

Chambers, Ciara, *Ireland in the Newsreels* (Dublin: Irish Academic Press, 2012).

Chapman, James, *The British at War: Cinema, State and Propaganda, 1939–45* (London: I.B Tauris, 1998).

Chapman, James, *Past and Present: National Identity and the British Historical Film* (London: I.B. Tauris, 2005).

Chapman, James, *Film and History* (Basingstoke: Palgrave Macmillan, 2013).

Chapman, James, Glancy, Mark and Harper, Sue, *The New Film History: Sources, Methods, Approaches* (New York and Basingstoke: Palgrave Macmillan, 2007).

Chiball, Steve and Murphy, Robert (eds.), *British Crime Cinema* (London: Routledge, 1999).

Colman, Felicity (ed.), *Film, Theory and Philosophy: The Key Thinkers* (Durham, NC: Acumen, 2009).

Cook, Pam, *Fashioning the Nation: Costume and Identity in British Cinema* (London: BFI Publishing. 1996).

Cook, Pam and Bernink, Mieke, *The Cinema Book*, 2nd edition (London: BFI Publishing, 1999).

Corrigan, Timothy J., *A Short Guide to Writing About Film* (New York and London: Pearson Longman, 2007).

Corrigan, Timothy and White, Patricia, *The Film Experience: An Introduction* (Boston: Bedford/St Martin's, 2009).

Creeber, Glen, *Tele-visions: An Introduction to Studying Television* (London: BFI Publishing, 2006).

Dickinson, Margaret and Street, Sarah, *Cinema and State: The Film Industry and the British Government 1927–1984* (London: BFI Publishing, 1985).

Drazin, Charles, *The Finest Years: British Cinema of the 1940s* (London: I.B. Tauris, 2007).

Dyer, Richard, *The Matter of Images: Essays in Representation* (London: Routledge, 1993).

Ede, Laurie N., *British Film Design: A History* (London: I.B. Tauris, 2010).

Egan, Kate, *Trash or Treasure? Censorship and the Changing Meaning of the Video Nasties* (Manchester: Manchester University Press, 2007).

Ellis, Jack C., *History of Film* (Boston, MA, and London: Allyn and Bacon, 1995).

Flanagan, Martin, *Bakhtin and the Movies: New Ways of Understanding Hollywood Film* (Basingstoke: Palgrave Macmillan, 2009).

Foster, Janet and Sheppard, Julia (eds.), *British Archives: A Guide to Archive Resources in the United Kingdom* (Basingstoke: Palgrave, 2002).

Gerarghty, Christine, *British Cinema in the Fifties: Gender, Genre and the 'New Look'* (London: Routledge, 2000).

Gibbs, John, *Mise-en-Scene: Film Style and Interpretation* (London: Wallflower Press, 2001).

Gifford, Denis, *British Film Catalogue: Fiction Film 1895–1994, Volume 1,* 3rd edition (London: Fitzroy Dearborn, 2001).

Gillham, Bill, *The Research Interview* (London: Continuum, 2000).

Glancy, Mark H., *When Hollywood Loved Britain: The Hollywood British Film, 1939–45* (Manchester: Manchester University Press, 1999).

Gocsik, Karen and Barsam, Richard, *Writing About Movies* (New York: Norton, 2007).

Grainge, Paul, Jancovich, Mark and Monteith, Sharon, *Film Histories: An Introduction and Reader* (Edinburgh: Edinburgh University Press, 2007).

Green, Anna and Troup, Kathleen, *The Houses of History: A Critical Reader in Twentieth-Century History and Theory* (Manchester: Manchester University Press, 1999).

Grenville, J.A.S., *Film as History* (Birmingham: University of Birmingham Press, 1971).

Hanson, Stuart, *From Silent Screen to Multi-Screen: A History of Cinema Exhibition in Britain since 1896* (Manchester: Manchester University Press, 2007).

Harper, Sue, *Picturing the Past: The Rise and Fall of the British Costume Film* (London: BFI Publishing, 1994).

Harper, Sue, *Women in British Cinema: Mad, Bad and Dangerous to Know* (London: Continuum, 2000).

Harper, Sue and Porter, Vincent, *British Cinema of the 1950s: The Decline of Deference* (Oxford: Oxford University Press 2003).

Harper, Sue and Smith, Justin (eds.), *British Film Culture in the 1970s: The Boundaries of Pleasure* (Edinburgh: Edinburgh University Press, 2011).

Haskell, Molly, *From Reverence to Rape: The Treatment of Women in the Movies*, 2nd edition (Chicago: University of Chicago Press, 1987).

Hibbin, Sally and Hibbin, Nina, *What a Carry On: Official Carry On Movie Book* (London: Hamlyn 1988).

Higson, Andrew, *Film England: Culturally English Filmmaking Since the 1990s* (London: I.B. Tauris, 2011).

Hill, John, *Sex, Class and Realism: British Cinema 1956–1963* (London: BFI Publishing, 1986).

Hill, John, *British Cinema in the 1980s: Issues and Themes* (Oxford: Clarendon Press, 1999).

Holmes, Su, *British TV and Film Culture of the 1950s: Coming to a TV Near You!* (Bristol: Intellect, 2005).

Hughes-Warrington, Marnie (ed.), *History on Film Reader* (Abingdon: Routledge, 2009).

Hughes-Warrington, Marnie, *History Goes to the Movies: Studying History on Film* (Abingdon: Routledge, 2007).

Hunt, Leon, *British Low Culture: From Safari Suits to Sexploitation* (London: Routledge. 1998).

Hutchings, Peter, *Hammer and Beyond: The British Horror Film* (Manchester: Manchester University Press, 1993).

Huxley, Aldous, *The Devils of Loudun* (London: Chatto & Windus, 1952).

Huzinga, Johan, *Men and Ideas: History, the Middle Ages and Renaissance*, trans. James S. Holmes and Hans van Marle (London: Eyre and Spottiswoode, 1960).

Jancovich, Mark, Faire, Lucy and Stubbings, Sarah, *The Place of the Audience: Cultural Geographies of Film Consumption* (London: BFI Publishing, 2003).

Jordanova, Ludmilla, *History in Practice* (London: Hodder Headline, 2000).

Kracauer, Siegfried, *From Caligari to Hitler: A Psychological Study of the German Film* (Princeton, NJ, and Oxford: Princeton University Press, 2004).

Kuhn, Annette, *Women's Pictures: Feminism and Cinema* (London: Routledge and Kegan Paul, 1982).

Kuhn, Annette, *Cinema, Censorship and Sexuality, 1909–25* (London: Routledge, 1988).

Lamberti, Ed (ed.), *Behind the Scenes at the BBFC: Film Classification from the Silver Screen to the Digital Age* (London: BFI Publishing/Palgrave Macmillian, 2012).

Landy, Marcia (ed.), *The Historical Film: History and Memory in Media* (New Brunswick, NJ: Rutgers University Press, 2000).

Leach, Jim, *British Film* (Cambridge: Cambridge University Press, 2004).

Low, Rachael *The History of British Film*, 7 vols (London and New York: Routledge, 1997; originally published Allen & Unwin, 1948).

Machin, David and Mayr, Andrea, *How to Do Critical Discourse Analysis: A Multimodal Introduction* (London: Sage, 2012).

McFarlane, Brian, *The Encyclopaedia of British Film*, 3rd edition (London: Methuen, 2008).

McKernan, Luke (ed.), *Yesterday's News: The British Cinema Newsreel Reader* (London: BUFVC Press, 2002).

Medhurst, Andy, *A National Joke: Popular Comedy and English Cultural Identities* (Abingdon: Routledge, 2007).

Metz, Christian, *Film Language: A Semiotics of the Cinema*, trans. Michael Taylor (Chicago: University of Chicago Press, 1991; originally published Oxford: Oxford University Press, 1974).

Monaco, James, *How to Read a Film: The World of Movies, Media and Multimedia: Language, History, Theory* (New York and Oxford: Oxford University Press, 2000).

Monk, Claire and Sargeant, Amy (eds.), *British Historical Cinema* (London: Routledge, 2002).

Mulvey, Laura, *Visual and Other Pleasures* (Basingstoke: Macmillan, 1989).

Murphy, Robert, *Realism and Tinsel: Cinema and Society in Britain 1939–48*, 2nd edition (London: Routledge, 1992).

Murphy, Robert, *British Cinema of the 90s* (London: BFI Publishing, 2000).

Murphy, Robert, *British Cinema and the Second World War* (London: Continuum, 2000).

Murphy, Robert, *The British Cinema Book*, 2nd edition (London: BFI Publishing, 2001).

Murphy, Robert, *Sixties British Cinema* (London: BFI Publishing, 2008).

Newland, Paul (ed.), *Don't Look Now: British Cinema in the 1970s* (Bristol: Intellect, 2010).

Newland, Paul, *British Films of the 1970s* (Manchester: Manchester University Press, 2013).

Nichols, Bill, *Movies and Methods: An Anthology*, vols 1 and 2 (Berkeley, CA, and London: University of California Press, 1976).

Ó Dochartaigh, Niall, *Internet Research Skills: How to Do your Literature Search and Find Research Information Online* (Los Angeles: Sage, 2007).

Orpen, Valerie, *Film Editing: The Art of the Expressive* (London: Wallflower Press, 2003).

Pears, Richard and Shields, Graham, *Cite them Right: The Essential Referencing Guide*, 9th edition (Basingstoke: Palgrave Macmillan, 2013).

Pereboom, Maartin, *History and Film: Moving Pictures and the Study of the Past* (Upper Saddle River, NJ: Pearson, 2010).

Petley, Julian, *Film and Video Censorship in Modern Britain* (Edinburgh: Edinburgh University Press, 2011).

Petrie, Duncan, *The British Cinematographer* (London: BFI Publishing, 1996).

Powell, Danny, *Studying British Cinema: The 1960s* (New York: Auteur Press, 2009).

Propp, Vladimir, *The Russian Folktale*, ed. and trans. Sibelan Forrester, foreword by Jack Zipes (Detroit: Wayne State University Press, 2012).

Pucci, Suzanne R. and Thompson, James, *Jane Austen and Co: Remaking the Past in Contemporary Culture* (Albany, NY: State University of New York Press, 2003).

Richards, Jeffrey, *The Age of the Dream Palace: Cinema and Society 1930–1939* (London: Routledge and Kegan Paul, 1984).

Robertson, James C., *The Hidden Cinema: British Film Censorship in Action, 1913–1975* (London: Routledge, 1993).

Robson, Colin, *How to Do a Research Project: A Guide for Undergraduate Students* (Oxford: Blackwell, 2007).

Rosenstone, Robert A., *History on Film/Film on History* (Harlow: Pearson, 2012).

Rudestam, Kjell and Newton, Rae, *Surviving your Dissertation: A Comprehensive Guide to Content and Process*, 3rd edition (London: Sage, 2007).

Sargeant, Amy, *British Cinema: A Critical History* (London: BFI Publishing, 2005).

Sedgwick, John, *Popular Filmgoing in 1930s Britain: A Choice of Pleasures* (Exeter: University of Exeter Press, 2000).

Sedgwick, John and Pokorny, Michael (eds.), *An Economic History of Film* (London: Routledge, 2005).

Shail, Robert (ed.), *Seventies British Cinema* (London: BFI Publishing/ Palgrave Macmillan, 2008).

Smith, Justin, *Withnail and Us: Cult Films and Film Cults in British Cinema* (London: I.B. Tauris, 2010).

Smith, Paul (ed.), *Film and the Historian* (Cambridge: Cambridge University Press, 1976).

Sorlin, Pierre, *The Film in History: Restaging the Past* (Basil Blackwell: Oxford, 1980).

Spicer, Andrew, *Typical Men: Representations of Masculinity in the Popular British Culture* (London: I.B. Tauris, 2001).

Stacey, Jackie, *Stargazing: Hollywood Cinema and Female Spectatorship* (London: Routledge, 1994).

Stam, Robert (ed.), *Film Theory: An Introduction* (Malden, MA: Blackwell, 2000).

Stokes, Melvyn and Maltby, Richard (eds.), *American Movie Audiences : From the Turn of the Century to the Early Sound Era* (London: BFI Publishing, 1999).

Street, Sarah, *British National Cinema* (London: Routledge: 1997).

Street, Sarah, *British Cinema in Documents* (London: Routledge, 2000).

Stubbs, Jonathan, *Historical Film: A Critical Introduction* (London: Bloomsbury, 2013).

Thompson, Kristin, *Storytelling in the New Hollywood: Understanding Classical Narrative Technique* (Cambridge, MA: Harvard University Press, 1999).

Tosh, John, *The Pursuit of History*, 4th edition (Harlow: Pearson Education, 2006).

Trevelyan, John, *What the Censor Saw* (London: Michael Joseph, 1973).

Walker, Alexander, *Hollywood England: The British Film Industry in the 1960s*, 2nd edition (London: Harrap, 1986).

Walker, John, *Once and Future Film: British Cinema in the Seventies and Eighties* (London: Methuen, 1985).

Walliman, Nicholas, *Your Research Project: A Step-by-step Guide for the First-time Researcher* (London: Sage, 2000).

Walliman, Nicholas, *Your Undergraduate Dissertation: The Essential Guide for Success* (London: Sage, 2004).

Wheatley, Helen, *Re-viewing Television History: Critical Issues in Television Historiography* (London: I.B. Tauris, 2007).

Williams, Raymond, *Culture and Society 1780–1950* (Harmondsworth: Penguin, Chatto & Windus, 1961).

Williams, Raymond, *Problems in Materialism and Culture* (London: Verso/NLB, 1980).

Wistrich, Enid, *'I Don't Mind the Sex, it's the Violence': Film Censorship Explored* (London: Marion Boyars Publishers, 1978).

CHAPTERS IN EDITED VOLUMES

Hughes, William, 'The evaluation of film as evidence' in Paul Smith (ed.), *Film and the Historian* (Cambridge: Cambridge University Press, 1976), pp. 49–71.

Petley, Julian, 'Us and them' in Martin Barker and Julian Petley (eds.), *Ill Effects: The Media Violence Debate*, 2nd edition (London: Routledge, 2001), pp. 87–101.

Richards, Jeffrey, 'Rethinking British cinema' in Justine Ashby and Andrew Higson (eds.), *British Cinema: Past and Present* (Abingdon: Routledge, 2000), pp. 21–34.

Richards, Jeffrey, 'Film and TV: the moving image' in Sarah Barber and Corinna M. Penniston-Bird (eds.), *History Beyond the Text: A Student's Guide to Approaching Alternative Sources* (London: Routledge, 2009), pp.72–86.

Rosenstone, Robert A., 'History in images/history in words' in Marnie Hughes-Warrington (ed.), *History on Film Reader* (Abingdon: Routledge, 2009) pp. 30–41.

Sorlin, Pierre, 'The film in history' in Marnie Hughes-Warrington (ed.), *History on Film Reader* (Abingdon: Routledge, 2009), pp. 15–16.

Zemon Davis, Natalie, 'Any resemblance to persons living or dead: Film and the challenge of authenticity' in Marnie Hughes-Warrington (ed.), *History on Film Reader* (Abingdon: Routledge, 2009), pp. 17–29.

JOURNAL ARTICLES

James, Robert, '*Kinematograph Weekly* in the 1930s: trade attitudes towards audience taste', *Journal of British Cinema and Television* 3:2 (2006), 229–243.

Mulvey, Laura, 'Visual pleasure and narrative cinema', *Screen* 16:3 (1975), 6–18.

Spicer, Andrew, 'The production line: reflections on the role of the producer in British cinema', *Journal of British Cinema and Television* 1:1 (November 2004), 33–50.

ONLINE ARTICLES

BBFC, 'Audiences and receptions of sexual violence in contemporary cinema', BBFC, 2 October 2007, http://bbfc.co.uk/what-classification /research (accessed 14 October 2014).

Bradby, Barbara, 'Our affair with Mila Kunis: a group ethnography of cinema-going and the "male gaze"', *Participations: Journal of Audience and Perception Studies* 10:1 (May 2013), www.participations.org/Volume %2010/Issue%201/2%20Bradby10.1.pdf (accessed 14 October 2014).

Hills, Matt, 'Fiske's "textual productivity" and digital fandom: Web 2.0 democratization versus fan distinction?', *Participations: Journal of Audience and Perception Studies* 10:1 (May 2013), www.participations. org/Volume%2010/Issue%201/9%20Hills%2010.1.pdf (accessed 14 October 2014).

Pett, Emma, '"Hey! Hey! I've seen this one, I've seen this one. It's a classic!": nostalgia, repeat viewing and cult performance in *Back to the Future*', *Participations: Journal of Audience and Perception Studies* 10:1 (May 2013), www.participations.org/Volume%2010/Issue%201/11%20Pett%20 10.1.pdf (accessed 14 October 2014).

von Tunzelmann, Alex, 'The Other Boleyn Girl: Hollyoaks in fancy dress', *Guardian*, 7 August 2008, www.guardian.co.uk/film/2008/ aug/07/1?INTCMP=SRCH (accessed 14 October 2014).

Whitlock, Cathy, 'The grand estates and castles of period moves', *Architectural Digest* online, www.architecturaldigest.com/ad/set-design/2013/ period-movies-set-design-manors-castles-vanity-fair-jane-eyre-article (acessed 15 October 2014).

ONLINE JOURNALS

BFI Screenonline, www.screenonline.org.uk.

Cineaste, www.cineaste.com.

Film Studies for Free, http://filmstudiesforfree.blogspot.co.uk.

Moving Image Source, www.movingimagesource.us.

Participations: Journal of Audience and Perception Studies, www.participations.org.

Variety, http://variety.com.

Vertigo, www.closeupfilmcentre.com/vertigo_magazine.

RESOURCES

BBC Written Archives Centre
Peppard Road
Caversham Park
Reading
RG4 8TZ
UK
Phone: 0118 948 6281
Email: heritage@bbc.co.uk
Web: www.bbc.co.uk/historyofthebbc/contacts/wac

British Board of Film Classification
3 Soho Square
London
W1D 3HD
UK
Phone: 0207 4401570.
Web: www.bbfc.co.uk/education-resources/book-visit-bbfc-archives

British Film Institute Reuben Library
BFI Southbank
Belvedere Road
South Bank
London
SE1 8XT
UK
Web: www.bfi.org.uk/education-research/bfi-reuben-library

British Library
96 Euston Road
London
NW1 2DB
UK
Phone: 01937 546060
Email: Customer-Services@bl.uk
Web: www.bl.uk

British Universities Film & Video Council
77 Wells Street
London
W1T 3QJ
UK
Phone: 020 7393 1500
Email: ask@bufvc.ac.uk
Web: www.bufvc.ac.uk

Harry Ransom Center
University of Texas at Austin
300 West 21st Street
Austin
Texas 78713-7219
USA

Phone: (512) 471-8944
Web: www.hrc.utexas.edu/collections/film

Imperial War Museum (London)
Lambeth Road
London
SE1 6HZ
UK
Phone: 020 7416 5000
Email: mail@iwm.org.uk
Web: www.iwm.org.uk

The National Archives
Kew
Richmond
Surrey
TW9 4DU
UK
Phone: 020 8876 3444
Web: www.nationalarchives.gov.uk

Margaret Herrick Library
Fairbanks Center for Motion Picture Study
333 South La Cienega Blvd
Beverly Hills
California 90211
USA
Phone: (310) 247 3020
Web: www.oscars.org/library

UCLA Film and Television Archive
UCLA Campus
Archive Research and Study Center (ARSC)
46 Powell Library
Los Angeles
California 90095
USA
Phone: (310) 206 5388
Email: arsc@cinema.ucla.edu
Web: www.cinema.ucla.edu

Hollywood Campus
1015 N. Cahuenga Blvd
Hollywood
California 90038
USA
Phone: (323) 462 4921
Web: www.cinema.ucla.edu

Online archives and holdings

BECTU, www.uea.ac.uk/film-television-media/research/research-themes/
british-film-and-tv-studies/british-cinema/oral-history-project.
British Pathé, www.britishpathe.com.
EUscreen, www.euscreen.eu.
European Film Gateway, www.europeanfilmgateway.eu.
Film Archives UK, http://filmarchives.org.uk.
Huntley Film Archive, www.huntleyarchives.com.
Movietone, www.movietone.com/n_Index.cfm.
Moving Image Archive, https://archive.org/details/movies.

INDEX